ENLIGHTENMENT
BLUES

PRAISE FOR ENLIGHTENMENT BLUES

"Andre van der Braak's writing is fresh and innocent. He describes with humor and reflection what really happens to those of us who offer themselves so completely to another human being. There are mystical experiences; the heights come to life, but also the pits, the awful cruelty of those who have given up their personal conscience. I found this book compelling and terrifying at the same time."
Orit Sen-Gupta, co-author of *Dancing the Body of Light - The Future of Yoga*

"*Enlightenment Blues* is the personal story of one man's eleven year journey into and out of a group of seekers of enlightenment with a charismatic leader who claims to be an exemplar of perfection. What distinguishes this book are the writer's insights and honesty. Anyone who has ever belonged to such a group, or knows anyone who has, or who wants to understand what the appeals and dangers of surrendering to a guru consist of, would benefit from reading this book."   Joel Kramer, co-author of *The Guru Papers*

"This is an important book. Read it. Andre's experience of falling for the Teacher's charming logic and his painful exploration of understanding the golden cage of teachers and teachings will be a useful story for many."   Mark Whitwell, author of *Yoga of Heart*

"Andre van der Braak's book, *Enlightenment Blues*, is an astounding and fascinating account of the eleven years he spent with his guru, Andrew Cohen. It tells of one human being's attempt, in the name of enlightenment, to compel another human being into abject submission. I saw how it was done. I was there. With an honesty that takes your breath away, the author reveals his own slow disintegration in the face of his master's ever growing paranoia and ferocious will to control. A splendid job."
Luna Tarlo, author of *The Mother of God*

Enlightenment Blues

MY YEARS WITH AN AMERICAN GURU

Andre van der Braak

MONKFISH BOOK PUBLISHING COMPANY
RHINEBECK, NEW YORK

Monkfish Memoirs 2

Library of Congress Cataloging-in-Publication Data

Braak, Andre van der, 1963-
Enlightenment blues : my years with an American guru / by Andre van
der Braak.-- 1st ed.
p. cm.
ISBN 0-9726357-1-8 (pbk.)
1. Braak, Andre van der, 1963- 2. Religious biography. I. Title.
BL73.B72A3 2003
299'.93--dc22   2003016323

Book and cover design by Georgia Dent

Cover art by René Magritte
Used with permission from ARS

Bulk purchase discounts, for educational or promotional purposes, are
available. Contact the publisher for more information.

First edition

First impression

10 9 8 7 6 5 4 3 2 1

Monkfish Book Publishing Company
27 Lamoree Road
Rhinebeck, NY 12572
www.monkfishpublishing.com

Some of the names and identifying characteristics of people have been
changed to protect their privacy.

To Sariputra and Mogallana

ACKNOWLEDGMENTS

I want to thank my publisher and editor Paul Cohen for the extraordinary amount of effort he put into making this book possible. I'm very grateful to Orit Sen-Gupta for her invaluable moral support throughout and her editing assistance with the difficult 'last leg'. I want to thank the ex-students of Andrew Cohen who have contributed to this story and who've read early drafts of this manuscript. But especially I want to thank Ute Wohlmuther, for being my companion during the five years that this book has been in the making. Without her love and support I would never have finished it.

TABLE OF CONTENTS

INTRODUCTION

All religions point to the same transpersonal truth. The realization of this truth is often indicated by the term 'enlightenment'.

Over the centuries many kinds of approaches have been devised to gain access to that larger truth. One thing they almost all have in common is the need to submit to a spiritual guide or teacher. This is deemed necessary because most of us are too caught up in our conditioning to find our own way out of it. Consequently for the teacher to be effective, the student must trust him or her very deeply.

A profusion of such minded spiritual communities exploded onto the scene during the Sixties and Seventies. As the churches in the West emptied out, the holy sites in the East filled up with westerners hungry for spiritual experiences. A spiritual renaissance was in the air. Westerners enrobed as Buddhist monks, visited ashrams to study yoga, and became followers of westernized Eastern teachers such as as Bhagwan Rajneesh, Chögyam Trungpa Rinpoche, Suzuki Roshi, or Swami Muktananda. Enlightenment seemed at hand.

At the time when my story begins, around the late eighties, the atmosphere had changed. The new goddess Enlightenment was not so easily won. Some of the original enthusiasm had given way to doubt and uncertainty. Buddhist monks disrobed and became meditation teachers in the West. They experimented with psychotherapy, romantic relationship as a spiritual path, and spirituality in daily life. The grandiose ambitions of before were scaled down to more realistic proportions. After the ecstasy, the laundry — as one book title puts it.

Apart from the elusive nature of enlightenment there was another disturbing development. Enlightened spiritual teachers had become embroiled in public scandals, usually related to sex, money or power. This left many dedicated spiritual seekers disappointed and disillusioned. Either enlightenment wasn't to be attained, or if it was attained, it didn't turn people into decent humans. There was a general sense of crisis and confusion.

In came Andrew Cohen, a fresh young American boy-next-door who had apparently managed to woo the ever-elusive Enlightenment. In 1986, after having tried many approaches, Andrew went to see an obscure Indian guru, H.W.L. Poonja, a disciple of the famous sage Ramana Maharshi. After a few conversations, the inconceivable happened. Enlightenment descended upon Andrew. In some mysterious way, Andrew had spontaneously morphed from an insecure thirty-year-old into a charismatic spiritual teacher with a silver tongue, exuding great clarity and a mystical presence. Suddenly Andrew was irresistible, and wherever he went people wanted to be around him, and hang onto his every word. He seemed to possess an uncanny ability to transmit a deep glimpse of enlightenment, inspiring people to leave everything behind and become his disciples. Thousands of people still full of hope and longing flocked to see him. When Andrew came to Amsterdam in 1987, I went to see him. Meeting Andrew was a revelation for me. I felt, like so many others around me, that finally I had understood what enlightenment was, not as a theory but as a living actuality. Those of us drawn to Andrew were also drawn to each other. We were united by a deep love for and surrender to Andrew. We saw ourselves as the latest manifestation of an age-old phenomenon, like Christ and his disciples, stirring up the religious (in this case Buddhist) establishment. We saw Andrew as a "fisher of men" who told us to "let the dead bury the dead." We were sure that Andrew's revolution would take the spiritual world by storm.

Andre van der Braak, July 2003

1

THE HONEYMOON

The foundation of spiritual life is clarity of intention.
Do I really want to be Free, here and now?

-Andrew Cohen

1.1. Meeting With Andrew

It is dead quiet in the small living room. I am in one of these squatting houses, small, decrepit but clean. The furniture has been removed from the living room — thirty people sit cross-legged on meditation cushions on the floor. Five people on chairs sit in the back watching. Nobody moves. Some have their eyes closed, others open. Everyone seems filled with a deep peace and rest. I've come here with my friend Harry who, fully engaged as usual, sits in one of the first rows while I sit on a chair in the back, checking things out from a distance.

The front door opens and closes. I hear coats rustling in the wardrobe, footsteps and then a disarming, friendly, smiling, young man steps into the room. He looks about thirty, six years older than me. A meditation cushion has been prepared for him in front of the room and he sits down cross-legged, facing everyone. Still smiling, he looks around the room, nodding hello to this person and the other. He has an open face, sensual mouth, a moustache, and black hair. His dark brown eyes possess something unusual, I don't know what exactly. He appears completely at ease, seemingly unaware that thirty people have their attention fixated on him. It's as if he's alone in his own living room. I take a liking to him immediately — a man without pretense. I am curious as to what will follow.

Andrew has completed his wordless greeting and sits still with closed eyes on his cushion. I wait for the program to start. After ten minutes I get the niggling feeling that I'm the only one in the room who's waiting for something. The others seem perfectly at ease, enjoying the silence. Then I realize there is no evening program! This is it! I sit up straight and close my eyes to meditate, which is not that difficult for me after five years of intensive Buddhist meditation practice. I scrupulously observe the rising and falling of the lower abdomen with each inhalation and exhalation. Thoughts that arise I put aside gently. I become quieter and quieter. A silence envelopes the room.

After two hours I hear rustling. When I open my eyes I see Andrew get up from his cushion and walk out of the room slowly. During the whole evening not a single word has been uttered. I am somewhat disappointed. So this was it? What about enlightenment? I did have a nice meditation though.

In the tram home Harry and I talk about the evening. Harry is enthusiastic. "Did you feel that energy?" he says. "Very strong. The energy of enlightenment."

I hesitate. I wouldn't go that far. But after all, I was sitting in the back row, not in the front.

"Yes, I did have a deep meditation," I allow him.

"Tomorrow there's satsang again," he says. "We have to get there early so we can sit in the front." Satsang is the Indian name for the public gatherings with Andrew. In Sanskrit it means "company with the wise", and is the customary term for the meetings of a spiritual teacher with his followers.

The next evening we both sit on the floor. Andrew is talking to people. Many have already been here before, some coming from abroad to Amsterdam — an impressive display of loyalty. Someone is asking Andrew what enlightenment is. I perk up my ears.

"Enlightenment," Andrew says with a smile, "is relief. It is cessation. It is the end of becoming. It's the end of the struggle to become anyone or anything. It's coming finally to rest, here and now, in this life."

That's not the kind of answer I expected. What is Andrew actually saying? Is he actually saying anything? My philosophically trained mind tries to extract some content from this proposition but doesn't get very far. Coming to rest, yes, but why do you come to rest then? And is life really such a struggle? Do I experience it as a struggle? Am I looking for relief? Andrew himself looks very serene, as if that relief has taken place for him already. He looks perfectly at ease. He's not holding some kind of lecture here; his words are based on what he is experiencing.

Andrew looks at the questioner with a faint smile, as if he wants to say, "Yes, it is that simple. I'm sorry I can't make it any more complicated." The questioner is looking into Andrew's eyes, and Andrew is looking back as if to say, "What now?" Not a word is exchanged. You could hear a pin drop in the room. I look from the questioner to Andrew and back. What is going on here? Some kind of deep alchemistic process, a transmission or something? Several moments go by.

Then the questioner bursts out laughing.

"That's it," Andrew calls out, "you got it. You just got it. You can't get enlightenment with the mind. What's your experience right now?"

The questioner, still laughing, cheerfully shrugs his shoulders. Others in the room also begin to laugh.

Andrew asks, "Is there any struggle right now?" The questioner shakes no. "Do you feel the need to become anyone or anything?" Again no.

"That's it," says Andrew. "Don't forget this." Then he continues to the rest of the room: "Did you see this? This man was trying to get a definition of enlightenment, something to take back home to chew on. But enlightenment goes beyond definition, goes beyond thought. You can only experience it directly, if you dare to let go of your thinking mind for a moment."

Everyone nods in agreement, and looks at the questioner. I look at him too. He looks like he's reborn. His eyes are radiant, and he has a permanent smile on his face. What just happened? Did Andrew stop his thinking mind with his unexpected answer? Did he transmit the essence of enlightenment to him?

Another fragment of a conversation touches me:

"Where is your passion for liberation? Without passion for liberation there is no hope for liberation. Passion for liberation is your liberation, and if you surrender to that passion, become a slave of that passion, your fate will be sealed."

Andrew speaks with an amazing self-confidence. He radiates certainty and charisma. He doesn't speak about enlightenment; he *is* enlightenment, that's what his whole appearance expresses.

1.2. My Earlier Life

"Lord, I beseech Thee; give me strength and power to do what's right, to remain faithful to Thee no matter what happens. Lord, I ask Thee, give that Carla is in love with me too and that we can marry each other later. Lord, I love Thee with all my heart. I will give Thee all that Thou would ask. Amen."

This was one of the prayers that I sent up to God every night. I was eight years old. Being raised as a Roman Catholic, I solemnly promised Jesus that I would dedicate my life to him. At the same time I had firmly decided to marry my young love Carla, and I asked God for help in this matter. The inherent contradiction in this didn't bother me. In church I sang my heart out, and I often experienced a sense of mystical awe. At eight-thirty in the morning, when the school Mass was over, I would walk from church to school feeling absolutely safe. God was my best friend who was watching over me.

I was the oldest of four children in a middle-class family. I spent my youth in a small town fifteen miles outside of Amsterdam. I was a bright boy, good at school and sports, but socially awkward and often isolated. My isolation was exacerbated by the fact that I stuttered, and was often ridiculed by my peers. From the age of eight, I was hopelessly in love with my classmate Carla. I was an incurable romantic, a daydreamer. My romantic infatuation with Carla (unrequited) would last until I was sixteen.

Because of my frequent stuttering I was sent to a speech therapist when I was fourteen. With her, I not only practiced breathing exercises and relaxation techniques, we also had long conversations. I was full of questions about God, about how we should live, about what was truly important in life. I didn't want to lead what I felt was an ordinary life, where I would just decide on a career, then find a girl, marry, and have a family. I was looking for more. I wanted my life to mean something. I wanted to be immersed in higher matters.

At sixteen, a classmate introduced me to Transcendental Meditation (TM), a system of meditation designed by the Indian guru Maharishi Mahesh Yogi. TM consisted of sitting quietly for twenty minutes twice a day, repeating a mantra that would take you to a deeper level of consciousness. At seventeen, I came into contact with the writings of the Indian sage and freethinker Jiddu Krishnamurti. His teachings took away the last remainders of my Roman Catholic faith. I went to Saanen in Switzerland to hear him speak in person.

Krishnamurti spoke about the possibility of an inner freedom from conditioning, a life freed from illusion and ignorance by a transformation of consciousness. I was moved by his description of this ultimate possibility and decided that this was the only thing truly worth pursuing. Rather than studying mathematics, as I had planned, I decided to study psychology and philosophy at the University of Amsterdam.

After I had settled in Amsterdam, I went to a large spiritual center there and came into contact with various spiritual teachers, practices, and eastern ways of thinking. One of them was Advaita Vedanta, the Indian non-dualistic school of Hinduism, of which the Indian sage Ramana Maharshi is the best-known representative in the West. I was very fond of a Dutch teacher called Wolter Keers. He was a warm and unpretentious sixty-year-old man, who had held a high-ranking job in Brussels. He didn't look like my idea of a spiritual teacher: he chain-smoked and looked like anyone else you would meet in the street. He had been to India, had studied with a guru there, and his identification with his ego had fallen away. His enlightenment had been confirmed by the famous Advaita Vedanta guru Sri Nisargadatta Maharaj.

Wolter would teach me that, "Who you are can never be grasped by thought. Thought always functions in duality, in good and bad, high and low, real and unreal. It can never grasp that which is beyond all duality."

Time and again he would encourage me to give up trying to grasp with my mind what cannot be grasped. He would tell me to "contemplate deeply on the most basic feeling of being alive, the sense of 'I am'. Then take away 'I', and take away 'am', and you'll be free." My illusion of being a separate self who was experiencing all kinds of things was the only obstacle to freedom, he said. Just see through that illusion and drop it: that's enlightenment.

Once when I was visiting Wolter at his home, he had to go out to the doctor for a back treatment. I stayed behind in his garden, reading a book of Nisargadatta. It was hot outside and I felt tired because I hadn't slept much. Suddenly, while reading, everything fell away and I experienced a vastness I had never known before. My consciousness seemed to expand to embrace the entire universe, and I felt a deep peace. Nothing mattered anymore, everything was all right. I don't know for how long I sat there. When Wolter returned home I went back into the house with him. As I walked up the stairs I suddenly felt dizzy and everything went dark. When I woke up I was in a hospital bed. I felt happy and at peace. Wolter and my parents were standing next to my bed, looking worried. They told me I had had an epileptic attack. Further examination in the hospital found nothing unusual, and I have never had an epileptic attack since. Wolter told me that such an attack can sometimes be an attempt of the brain to wipe itself clean. Whatever it was, it scared me to death, and for several months I didn't dare close my eyes in meditation.

But soon my longing for enlightenment was stronger than my fears. When a year later Wolter suddenly died of a heart attack, I continued my spiritual search in other directions. Buddhism was speaking about enlightenment as well, that it was the way out of suffering. The Buddha had spoken about the Eightfold Path, a system of ethics and meditation that culminated in insight and wisdom. I became an ardent practitioner of Buddhist insight meditation, or vipassana. This type of meditation is training in mindfulness, being completely attentive to what is happening in the present moment. By continued mindfulness we attain the three most important insights into the nature of reality: that everything is inherently unsatisfactory, that everything is impermanent, and that any idea of a self, or a fixed essence, is an illusion. These insights free us from craving and ignorance, and we come to rest in enlightenment.

I became very involved. I lived in a student flat and at 6 a.m., when my housemates came home from a night of carousing, I got up to meditate. I practiced sitting and walking meditation for several hours a day and participated in meditation retreats of up to ten days. My Buddhist teacher gave me the Pali name of Suddhatta (purity).

One of my meditation buddies was Harry, a 28-year-old Dutchman. He had also been a spiritual seeker since he was 18. He had been involved with the Hare Krishna-movement, had traveled in India for years, almost died from liver disease in the process, and had discovered Buddhist meditation practice while in India. He was also following gestalt therapy training, and we spoke a lot together about psychology and enlightenment. In my studies of psychology and philosophy I was looking for a synthesis between East and West. In 1986, I wrote my psychology thesis comparing psychoanalysis and

Buddhist insight meditation, based on the ideas of the American thinker Ken Wilber. For my philosophy thesis I compared Nietzsche and Buddhism. But after graduation I yearned for a job in the real world, out of these high-minded theoretical realms. Since it was difficult to find a job as a philosopher or a psychologist, I started working as a computer consultant with NCR. I had worked with computers quite a bit at the university, and knew a lot about the Unix operating system.

Slowly both Harry and I were becoming disillusioned with our Buddhist meditation practice. Did all this meditation lead to anything? What was enlightenment actually? Did it even exist? Our teacher seemed none too eager to get into all these questions. He just wanted us to continue the practice. When we heard stories about the dubious ways he related to his female students we lost faith in him as a teacher. Harry then heard about an unknown young American who was rumored to be enlightened by an Indian guru. He was teaching Advaita Vedanta and would be holding public gatherings in the Staatsliedenbuurt in Amsterdam. Maybe this would be the answer to our questions.

1.3. Existential Crisis in Dayton: What Do I Really Want?

For two weeks, I sit night after night in the living room in the Staatsliedenbuurt, mostly on a chair in the back. I'm still checking things out. I enjoy the silence; it feels as if my brain is being burnt away.

Andrew is giving teachings largely through dialogue with others, about the Self, about the experience of knowing nothing and being no one. He talks about letting go of the ego so that we can become part of this deeper consciousness. The words seem to come straight from Emptiness itself. There is an atmosphere of silence, without pretense. Halfway through the evening, herb tea with a cookie is served. The very Dutch word "cozy" would almost be right here. I cherish this atmosphere like a warm bath.

I don't want to spoil that feeling by arguing with Andrew about his message, or losing myself in philosophical nitpicking. Actually I'm very shy for a reason unknown to me. Usually I have no problems finding words when it comes to philosophical and spiritual discussions. I feel somehow naked in this place, as if my deepest feelings are laid bare, at last unprotected by my intellect. There is something sacred about this atmosphere, something awe-inspiring, and I feel myself back in the church of my youth, absorbing the sacred full of awe.

Slowly I hear more about Andrew's background. Born in New York City in 1955, he had spent nearly his entire youth in psychoanalysis, which was followed by a spontaneous spiritual experience at 16. Over time, he became a restless spiritual seeker, practicing martial arts, Kundalini, Vipassana, but he couldn't find what he was after. Then he traveled to Lucknow, India, to meet a then little known 80-year-old Advaita Vedanta teacher Harilal Poonja. On the third day of their meeting Andrew had a powerful experience of awakening. Within three weeks of their initial meeting Poonja told Andrew "their work was over," so the story went. He sent Andrew out to go teach enlightenment in the West, to "create a revolution among the young," telling him that he was the son he had been waiting for all his life.

Almost immediately Andrew attracted students. His Indian girlfriend Alka, whom he would marry a year later, accepted him as her master early on. Andrew traveled on to Rishikesh, in northern India where he was met by several young Westerners who also became early students. They would hang out all day, sometimes staying up all night, talking about the miracle of enlightenment. Andrew then went to Devon, England, where he was invited to teach by a Buddhist friend. Many long term Buddhists in Devon, several of whom were meditation teachers, became students. They were very devoted and traveled far and wide to be with Andrew in satsang.

* * *

"What do you think is the most important thing to reach enlightenment?"

The young man is looking intently at Andrew.

"Well," Andrew says with a smile, "in the spiritual life it's most important to have clarity of intention. You have to ask yourself, 'What do I really want? What is really, when it comes down to it, the most important thing for me in my life?' Many people say they're interested in this thing called enlightenment, but do you really feel a passion for enlightenment?"

The young man shows some hesitation. Andrew continues, "Do you really want to be free more than anything else? Are you willing to give up anything for it? If that's really true for you, you won't have any trouble reaching enlightenment. Enlightenment will be right here and now for you." He speaks these last words with passion, and the room suddenly sparks with electricity.

The young man sits as if struck. He seems to be considering this possibility for the first time in his life. Give everything to enlightenment and sacrifice everything else. His eyes start to glow.

I sit as if transfixed on my cushion. I think back on all those years of meditation practice, striving for enlightenment as if it were some far away goal in the future. I consider myself a devoted and serious seeker, but how much have I been willing to give for enlightenment up until now? Hasn't my spiritual search been more of a convenient life style, a pleasant dressing up? What about my own passion for enlightenment? Then it comes like a thunderbolt: enlightenment has nothing to do with strategizing or some linear path of self-improvement. It is always here, now, this moment, this choice, this fire burning in my guts. This is where I have to act from, not my mind. My mind is only interested in enlightenment as some kind of self protection, to prevent me from actually ever encountering the real thing!

I witness many more conversations with Andrew. I see many seekers who've been on the path for many years, who've visited the ashrams in India, who've done the meditation practices — and still their hearts are longing for fulfillment. Now they see Andrew radiating the very thing they've been looking for all these years. And they hear Andrew say, "It can happen to you too! You don't need any special qualifications. You only have to want it badly enough." And then, when someone "gets it," Andrew points to him and shouts, "This is it, you've got it!"

I would love to continue sitting here night after night. But the world is still calling me. In two days, the plane awaits me. My employer is sending me to their education center in Dayton, Ohio for three months. There I will be saturated with courses on Unix, C, and data communication. At this point in time it might as well have been Swahili, it feels so removed from me as I am floating in this pool of silence.

Then Andrew suddenly speaks to me, "That man there in the back row, yes, with the glasses. You've been here before, right?"

I confirm that I have come every night for the past two weeks.

"Do you have any questions?"

I shake my head no.

"I think it's time that you and I break the sound barrier. Can you tell me a bit about yourself?"

I tell him that I work with computers and that I have to leave in two days for three months in Dayton. Andrew laughs and says Dayton is the most boring city in America, something like Liverpool. I laugh too, and the ice is broken between us. I've gotten past my shyness. I have gone from observer to participant.

* * *

I'm lying in the swimming pool of the Dayton Holiday Inn, a cool drink by my side. It is a hundred degrees outside but a soft cool breeze flows past my skin. I'm depressed. What am I doing here? Where is my life going? Am I going to pursue a career in computers, spend the rest of my life among squares and nerds? I can't see a path for myself in 'the world'. I'm not interested in getting rich, becoming famous, becoming a scholar. More often than not, my thoughts float back to those evenings with Andrew, the wonderful silence, the passion for enlightenment in that room. Yes, that's what I'm interested in. That's the only thing that gives me a thrill.

* * *

"This is Harry."

"Hi Harry, this is Andre. I'm calling from the States. I just wanted to say hello."

"Hi Andre. Good to hear you! Are you having a good time with your classes there?"

"Well, it's okay. I'm learning a lot."

"Well, you're also missing a lot! It's fantastic here. You won't believe what is happening around Andrew. It's a revolution. Every day more people are coming. And Andrew is so great, so natural, so spontaneous. I feel that all my questions are answered. We really wasted our time with Buddhism! We were so stupid. Only now do I see what enlightenment really means: total revolution, leaving everything behind, going into the unknown; very different from meditating an hour a day. I wish you were here to see it, Andre."

"Well, er, that sounds really good Harry."

"Sounds really good? It's revolution, Andre; it's the end of the known, living in the unknown. And you know what? Andrew's invited me to come with him to

Jerusalem, he's going there for six weeks to give satsang, but I have to hang up Andre, Andrew can come and visit any moment. Are you doing all right there? Come back soon! How long are you still there?"

"Three more weeks."

"Oh, then we'll still be gone when you come back to Holland. But I'll see you as soon as I come back from Jerusalem. Bye, lots of love."

With the receiver still in my hand I continue to stand for a while, overwhelmed by a torrent of emotions. The intensity of Harry's excitement and enthusiasm is in complete contrast with my own depressive state of decomposition. Is this the way out of my crisis? Harry is now with Andrew; he's not a Buddhist anymore. Am I still one? I try to sit down in the familiar posture, eyes closed, watching the breath. But it is as if the trick doesn't work anymore. I remain as restless and haunted as before. I feel the knot in my belly contract.

I am glad when I'm back on Dutch territory, but I can't find my rhythm. The crisis that I suffered in Dayton is not resolved. I find that I can't just step back into my old life, like putting on a suit that has hung in the closet for three months. It is as if the moths have been eating away at my life. I stay busy every day at my job, and my brain is absorbing all the newly received knowledge and putting it into practice. But in the back of my mind, I'm counting the days until Andrew and Harry are back.

One evening I'm sitting on the couch watching a Batman rerun when the doorbell rings. I open the door, and Harry storms into the room full of enthusiasm.

Happily, we fall into each other's arms. The knot in my stomach recedes into the background. Harry's looking so good, he's radiant and self-assured. Not like the old Harry that I knew. Even before he sits down on the couch, he has already plunged into the first of a long collection of stories about Jerusalem, about Andrew, and about the revolution. He is completely thrilled about Andrew and his message, and in fact he can't imagine what else in life could possibly be worthwhile. Harry clearly has found his destination in life.

Sitting opposite him on the couch, I reflect on the image that I have of Harry. He grew up in Schiedam, had a distant and dominant father and a sweet but submissive mother. He was supposed to take over his father's business, a chain of optical stores. He rebelled by becoming a macho biker, and then at twenty-one by travel to India, looking for peace, love and happiness. While there he meditated a lot but became very ill, nearly dying. In 1983, he had come back to Holland a wreck, and that's when I met him, when he joined our meditation group. A wreck is the last thing that Harry looks like now.

"Do you remember Sariputra and Mogallana, Andre?" Harry suddenly asks. I know what he means. Harry and I have grown to be Buddhist companions over the past years, and we always liked to compare ourselves to the famous Buddhist monks from the Pali scriptures, the intellectual Sariputra and the power person Mogallana. They were two friends looking for enlightenment, and went from one teacher to the other. They had an agreement that if one would discover the true teacher, he would warn the other right away. In this way they both joined the Buddha, and grew into the most venerated monks of the Buddhist Sangha (community). This is the story that Harry reminds me of now. As Mogallana Harry it is his spiritual duty to inform me, Sariputra Andre that the true teacher has no doubt come into our life. His name is Andrew Cohen.

1.4. Clarity of Intention Resolved: I Want to be Free

The satsangs start up again. I speak with Andrew about my experience in Dayton, the hotels and restaurants that were meaningless to me, the loneliness. He seems to understand it all.

"When you have a longing for liberation," he says, "you won't feel at home in the world of materialism. When everyone only thinks about chasing their own advantage, and is trying to become someone in the world, it's understandable that you don't feel at home there. Maybe it's a good idea to spend more time with like-minded people."

He asks me whether I've ever just "hung out" in my life. No, I haven't. He encourages me to consider that idea.

There's so much I have to ask Andrew about: enlightenment, Buddhism, spiritual practice. And what about having to make an effort to become enlightened? In answering this last question, Andrew looks at me directly with his penetrating brown eyes. After a few seconds of silence, he repeats to me what his own teacher told him, slowly stressing every word and the spaces between,

"You—do—not—have—to—make—*any*—effort—to— be—free." He almost whispers. We continue to look into each other's eyes. My mind is racing. Can this be true? Suddenly all movement stops, and the moment seems to expand into eternity. In this vast space that has suddenly opened up a thought presents itself: enlightenment is not an object. You can't strive after it or attain it. It is the very source of being itself, the source of my own existence. It's actually impossible not to be enlightened. It's only the stubborn arrogance of my mind that prevents me from seeing this simple truth. Andrew smiles at me then moves on to the next questioner. I sit as if in a daze. My mind stays empty for what seems like an eternity.

When the evening ends I ride home quietly on my bicycle. I feel a very new emotion arising within me. I am falling in love with Andrew. I have always respected my teachers, even to the point of veneration, but it was never love. When I look into Andrew's eyes I feel myself melt. My resistances are fading away, and I feel the way people usually feel about lovers—I want to be with him all the time.

When I'm with Andrew in satsang, I feel myself melt in a pool of absolute bliss, a place beyond good and evil, beyond conception itself. I feel he is in direct contact with the source of all being, the source prior to thought and feeling. It is the source in which I recognize myself, my own true face. Andrew takes me to this place where I no longer experience any separation or boundary between myself and others, between past, present or future, between pain and ecstasy. Andrew seems to radiate something that can counter all that is evil; that can put the mind to rest. To sit still together with Andrew brings a spontaneous meditation, no fight with thoughts and feelings; just a slow, irreversible absorption into the depths of consciousness. It all seems so spontaneous, so easy, and yet there is something powerful emanating from Andrew. I feel that higher forces are at work here.

Is this enlightenment that I'm experiencing? I hardly dare think so. Me, enlightened? But I can't deny that my whole being is shouting, *"This is it."* I feel completely at home with myself and with life. I feel an unbearable intimacy with the people around me in this room, an intimacy that I can only call love. I am not worried, deep inside in my guts I know that life is good, that there is no problem, there is peace. What more could I want? What else could there be to strive after? I only see perfection wherever I look. All the questions that I had in Dayton have been answered.

I tell Andrew that I'm considering following him to Devon. Does he think that's a good idea? "If that's what you want to do, that's fine," he says. "I'm not stopping you." I tell him about the fear that I'm also experiencing, the fear of leaving behind my house and my job, the fear of losing my life basically. "Don't expect the fear to go away" he says, laughing, "It will get a lot worse".

The next few days are agonizing. I keep asking, "Why would I give up my whole life in Amsterdam? What do I have to gain?" But the answer wells up in my heart with increasing clarity: "Happiness, peace, deep contentment; the answer to all my questions. Everything I've always looked for in my search for enlightenment.

I write Andrew a note:

"After all my years of spiritual practice I feel that enlightenment was never the number one priority in my life. Thank you for helping me to finally get my priorities straight. I have resolved my clarity of intention. I am looking forward to seeing you in Devon in September."

With the note I put a hundred guilders as a gift to help cover Andrew's expenses in Amsterdam. The next evening in satsang, on his way out, Andrew stops next to me, and shakes my hand, without saying anything. Then he walks on. We see eye to eye now. A few days later I invite Andrew to have dinner together, and he accepts. We go to an Indian restaurant and talk freely together. I tell him about my background in psychology and philosophy, he tells me about how he never got good grades in school and had always envied people that had those intellectual capacities. We have a lot of fun; there is a tangible intimacy, no trace of pretense or any hierarchical difference between us. It is like a date between two lovers. I am over the moon. If Andrew is truly the Buddha of our time, then I am now having a bowl of rice with the Buddha! What good fortune that I've met Andrew. What good fortune that he and I can be such good friends. What good fortune that the secret of enlightenment has finally been revealed to me.

1.5. Revolution in Devon, Amsterdam and Rome

In September 1987, Andrew leaves Amsterdam to go back to Devon. I take an unpaid leave from my job and go with him. Andrew teaches in the small town of Totnes, the center of a local new age scene. He lives in a small cottage belonging to a larger farmhouse called Beenleigh. Because the living room of the cottage is too small, a neighboring barn has been built into a satsang hall. There Andrew gives satsang six times a week. Soon, upwards of one hundred and fifty people are coming to hear him teach. We have to line up every night to get a good seat.

Life around Andrew in Devon is exciting. We feel like spiritual revolutionaries, shaking up the fossilized spiritual scene, especially the western Buddhist scene. Andrew challenges its complacency and corruption, speaking out against a certain status quo that has set in. It's as if the western meditation teachers no longer consider enlightenment an attainable goal. Some of them are now advocating psychotherapy in combination with meditation. Others are teaching relationship or parenting as a spiritual path. Andrew doesn't buy any of all this. He insists that enlightenment is beyond the mind and the ego, and that psychotherapy can only make the mind and ego stronger, more integrated, and healthier. He considers this a watering down of the spiritual teaching of enlightenment. He says spiritual life is not a hobby you can practice on the weekends or add to your life as a bonus. The spiritual life is a life of renunciation, and not compatible with a worldly view.

He challenges his former Buddhist meditation teacher to a dharma debate—and we feel he clearly wins. The new has won out over the old. Quite a few of the long-term Buddhist practitioners and even a few of the teachers become followers of Andrew. There's controversy in the air. Buddhist students are discouraged from going to Andrew's teachings. He is accused of hypnotizing his followers.

In his satsangs Andrew tries to inspire us to dedicate our life to the ecstatic reality of enlightenment, to surrender to our longing for liberation. The satsang room is often buzzing with excitement. After years of spiritual practice leading us nowhere, suddenly everything seems possible.

To stay in touch with Andrew, we write notes to him to tell him about our experiences, about how satsang has struck us. Often Andrew reads our notes aloud in satsang. If it happens to be our own letter we're ecstatic. We're a close-knit group. We see each other every night in satsang, and the rest of the time we do everything together: eating, talking, discussing Andrew's teachings, blissing out, watching videos, listening to music. There's an indescribable sense of intimacy between us. We're family.

Before long we're all writing ecstatic love letters full of mystical experiences and profound gratitude. We address Andrew as "beloved Master," just like Andrew did with his own teacher, Poonjaji. In our houses we have pictures of Andrew, so we never have to be without his disarming, boyish smile, and his beautiful eyes that radiate goodness. His gaze seems to come straight from the Beyond. There's none of us, man or woman, who isn't profoundly in love with Andrew. We can stare at his picture for long stretches of time, feel ourselves melt and become one with him. In such a state of surrender, life flows by effortlessly. There's no problem, nor has there ever been one, or could there ever be one. We're just letting go and relaxing into this state of surrender, again and again and again.

In the evening satsangs we're amazed by the profound clarity in each of Andrew's responses. He always hits the nail right on the head, puts his finger on some fixed idea that the questioner has unknowingly been carrying around, dissolves some emotional resistance in another, and sends us all into deep bliss through long and powerful silences, where we can feel the reality of No Separation tangibly penetrating the room.

During the day we walk around with this precious secret firmly established in our consciousness. We can see it in each other's eyes; we can hear it in any word we utter, whether in profound conversation or idle chitchat. Everything becomes sacred, whether it's having tea with scones in the local tearoom, listening to a Van Morrison tape, or watching a Marilyn Monroe comedy. It's the secret of enlightenment that we share, unbeknownst to the other inhabitants of Totnes, who to us seem to merely continue in their dreary, daily plodding existence, with no eyes to see and no ears to hear.

We've rented a house in Dittisham, a few kilometers from Dartmouth. It's a semi-detached. Ten of us live in the left house, seven of us in the right. Because Andrew comes to visit often, and shows an active interest in the affairs of the house, others consider us as a kind of inner circle. We ourselves feel that too.

I am utterly happy here. I have found my destiny, like water that reaches its true level. The past and the future have fallen away from me, and I'm living in an eternal now. It feels as if my personal biography is at an end, like a book that after a certain page only contains blank pages.

One of my housemates is a woman from Denmark named Sarah. She is 26. She has left her college studies to follow Andrew to England. She is attractive, intelligent and lively but also insecure. We spend a lot of time together, going for walks, having long conversations. I give her table tennis lessons during which we rave together about the fantastic turn that our lives have taken. Slowly we begin to feel attracted to each other. One day Sarah brings up the topic of being in a relationship together. I am not sure how this fits in with our new life. If my life is a book that contains only empty pages, how can I start to fill it up with other things? How would Andrew feel about this?

During the earlier days of Andrew's teaching, there had been touchy-feely stuff going on between people, something not that uncommon around certain kinds of gurus. People would stare into each other's eyes for a long time, titillating themselves and each other with feelings of bliss and intimacy. In such a state it would seem the most natural thing in the world to sleep with each other. But Andrew spoke out against such things. Promiscuity would only distract from the jewel of enlightenment. He wanted people to be either in a relationship or otherwise to behave themselves.

I decide to talk about it with Andrew. He listens to my story and then advises me to let it go for now. "You're just getting established in this new realization," he says, "and getting into a relationship would only distract you at this point."

I tell Sarah what Andrew has counseled and we decide to cool it, and just be friends.

In January 1988, Andrew goes back to Amsterdam to teach. From there it will be to Rome. A firm community member by now, I give him my apartment in Amsterdam for the month, while I live with five others in a one-bedroom apartment. Sarah is also there. And again Sarah and I become attracted to each other. Each night I give her a goodnight kiss, and this little ritual becomes a little more extended every night. Then one evening as the others are out and Sarah and I are home alone, our overheated nervous systems can contain themselves no longer, and we start kissing and making out on the couch. We are definitely in love, what to do? I write a letter to Andrew, telling him about our renewed attraction, and asking him for permission to get together in a relationship. His answer is something to the extent that we are free to do what we like. After Andrew has finished teaching in Amsterdam he moves on to Rome for a month, and Sarah and I move into my apartment.

Andrew's teachings in Rome are a true European gathering. Students flock from England, Holland, Germany, France, Austria, Switzerland, and of course Italy itself, enjoying the city, the fashion shops, and the coffee shops. It's one huge vacation for everyone. After two weeks in Amsterdam with Sarah, I go for two weeks to Rome, to be with everyone. I live in a large apartment with twenty others. Every evening there is satsang, and during the day we hang out in Rome. It is just like our life style in Devon, only the scenery has changed. We invite Andrew to have a coffee with us and he accepts. He asks me to pick him up. So, dressed up in my best clothes, I go over to his flat. Alka, now his wife, lets me in and says that Andrew is almost ready. Then Andrew steps into the room, fresh out of the shower, and starts dressing. We chat about all kinds of things, and when he's ready, we take a bus to the restaurant. On the bus I talk to him about my relationship with Sarah. In some kind of way I am trying to get his blessing for our relationship, but he is neutral and noncommittal. I am relieved that Andrew at least doesn't disapprove. And I am thrilled to be spending this private time with him. Like always, it's wonderful to be with him.

Satsang in Rome is a big success. The living room there is a lot bigger than the one in Amsterdam, but is still much too small for the hundred and fifty people who try to squeeze themselves into eighty square meters. We sit locked in shoulder to shoulder on the floor, listening attentively to Andrew. The temperature in the room reaches tropical heights. This, for now, is the last chance to come to satsang in Europe. Andrew has announced that he will move to Amherst, Massachusetts, next month. As soon as Andrew starts giving satsang in the U.S. he will draw thousands of people in no time. We're all convinced of that. Then we might all be sitting anonymously in the back row. So now is the time to take advantage of the attention we can still get from Andrew.

I sit cross-legged on the floor. I am in bliss. Andrew speaks about his own story with Poonjaji. In front of a large audience that is awed with admiration, he says that Poonjaji has told him he will create a revolution amongst the young in the West! "I pass my mantle on to you," Poonjaji had said. Andrew says that whoever wants can follow him to America where he will be teaching. From the first of May onwards, everyone is welcome in Amherst. A wave of excitement goes through the room. This will be the next chapter in the revolution! We will leave our lives in Europe behind and jump into the unknown in Amherst, burning up together in the fire of enlightenment.

2

You Have To Change

Everybody wants to be enlightened but nobody wants to change.

-Andrew Cohen

2.1. Amherst

Amherst, the small town in the middle of Massachusetts, home to five colleges including Smith, Holyoke, and the University of Massachusetts, is also an area where many western Buddhists live. Nearby, in the small town of Barre, is the prominent Insight Meditation Society where famous American Buddhist teachers such as Joseph Goldstein and Jack Kornfield teach. Andrew has been invited to teach in Amherst by a middle-aged American named Jacob who had been a Buddhist monk in Asia for six years, and had been meditating for twenty when he met Andrew, a meeting which has turned his life upside down just as it has mine.

In May 1988, with a few thousand dollars in my pocket, I fly there on a one-way ticket. Sarah stays in Amsterdam for another month to make some more money. There are about a hundred students in Amherst by the time I arrive. The college students have gone for the summer, so we live in the big fraternity houses in groups of ten or more. After Sarah arrives, she and I live with eight others in a house called The Yellow House. We settle into the familiar rhythm that we know so well from Devon.

Andrew gives satsang almost every evening in the living room of his large house. During the days we go to the beach, or for walks, or out for coffee with each other. We are from all parts of the world, and the most important thing that connects us is Andrew, his teachings, and the community that we are starting to form together. And that's mostly what we talk about. What did Andrew speak about last night? Who's been invited to cook for Andrew? The letters we write to him are another inexhaustible topic of conversation. Night after night we have powerful experiences of oneness and intimacy in satsang. They powerfully confirm for us that the revolution is under way. Although we live in different houses spread out over Amherst, it feels like we live in a single ashram. The town is ours. We are high on enlightenment all the time. To live in such ecstatic abandonment, with nothing to hold on to, is thrilling and terrifying at the same time.

As it turns out, the very insecurity and vulnerability of such a way of life seems to be too much to bear for some of us. I hear an unsettling story about Jacob. He is no longer there when I arrive. He apparently had a falling out with Andrew and left. From what I hear, Jacob was having doubts about Andrew and having difficulty surrendering. His ego must have come back in and pulled him back into familiar territory. It's a reminder to us all how important it is to have clarity of intention and to guard the precious realization of enlightenment against the poison of our mind.

And indeed living together with so many people from different countries and cultural backgrounds is not as easy as we expected, especially in this situation where the future is so completely open-ended. No one, including Andrew, knows where this is going. We have to trust and surrender. Although at the deepest level we feel everything is perfect, at the more mundane level of living together, some problems begin to develop. We find that in spite of our newly found recognition and celebration of enlightenment, most of us still behave in less than enlightened ways. For Andrew this is unacceptable. "Once you've realized the truth," he says, "you have to live up to it." So, no more neuroses, no more selfishness, no more temper tantrums. Get your act together. Andrew encourages us to have house meetings where we can come together and evaluate how we are doing.

In this way, Andrew's message begins to change. He still speaks about clarity of intention as the way to enlightenment, but he also begins to speak now about the need to make clear choices in day-to-day life, choices that will keep our enlightened state free from obstacles, such as attachments and conditioned patterns. And that could mean making very different choices than we have been making, whether out of psychological habit, laziness, or simple ignorance. Andrew calls this 'the law of volitionality'. It means total responsibility at all times. We are always free to choose, so we are also always responsible and accountable for what we choose. He starts to emphasize the need to change, which means letting go of the old conditioned tendencies and no longer acting out of them.

Having to change? I'm still utterly happy; nothing could be more perfect than it is now. So what needs to change? When I met Andrew I was profoundly relieved that I could be done with my Buddhist self-improvement program, meditating hours every day, inching my way towards final enlightenment, chipping away at my ego with every minute of meditation. There was no thrill there, no revolution, only spinning your wheels, one part of yourself trying to improve the other part. Andrew's message had been, nothing has to change, everything is perfect as it is, just realize this and surrender to it deeply and all your problems will be over. Your whole life will be over. So what is all this talk about having to change now? From what I've heard, Andrew's own teacher Poonja never speaks about having to change. Is Andrew going back to a Buddhist approach?

I share my concerns with Andrew in satsang.

"Oh well," he says, "it's not such a big deal. It's like housekeeping, taking care of business, cleaning up some old karma."

"But I thought enlightenment meant the end of all the old karma, the end of the road?"

"Well, yes, if you're lucky. That's how it happened for me. But apparently it's not that way for everybody. It's not like that with most of you, or so it seems, unfortunately. So then you just do what you have to do. You take responsibility for all the karma that's still there."

"But isn't that what I was doing as a Buddhist?"

"No, it's very different. Then you all the time felt that something was wrong, something was missing. Now you know for sure that nothing is wrong, and nothing is missing. And that should give you all the energy and the passion you need to change where you have to change."

"But what happened then with enlightenment being no limitation?"

"Well, there still is no limitation. We can all change at any moment. It doesn't have to take time. You don't need to do years of therapy, or meditate for years. You can just decide to change, like this!" Andrew snaps his fingers.

"Just by wanting to change, you mean?"

"Yes, but also by recognizing that everything is volitional. You always have a choice! You can always choose to do the right thing, and not to do the wrong thing. We know what's right and what's wrong. Once you've realized enlightenment, you can no longer plead ignorance. You can't say any longer what people usually say, "Well, I just didn't know any better."

"So by changing do we get more enlightened then?"

"No! Absolutely not. You see, enlightenment is not some gradual process in time. It's there, in a flash, when you realize it. It's an eternal reality beyond time and space that we can dip into at any time. You only need to have the guts to see your neuroses for what they are and take a leap beyond them into the unknown. Otherwise, what good would enlightenment be? If it doesn't lead to a beautiful human being, what's the point? You can't say 'that's just the way that I am.' You have to change. It's a moral obligation to life, to the cosmos itself. You have to align yourself with the standard of enlightenment."

But the standard of enlightenment proves to be difficult to meet. One by one, Andrew's housemates have to leave his house because they don't meet the standard. Kathy, an English girl who knew Andrew personally before his enlightenment, has to leave because she can be opinionated and have a bad temper. Alan, a fragile former hippie from New Zealand, has to leave because he is too fearful and insecure. Harry at this time is also living with Andrew. He tells me what it's like to live with Andrew in the house. "It's very intense," he says. "Because Andrew is immersed in enlightenment he can't bear any selfishness or impurity around him. Around Andrew all those kinds of impurities come ruthlessly to light, and you have to be prepared to give them up. You have to be willing all the time to dare to reach beyond your limits." When Harry tells me these things, I'm on the one hand jealous that he's so close to Andrew and that he has such a unique chance to have his impurities brought to light. On the other hand I find that I don't mind being a little further removed from that all-consuming fire, so that I can warm myself with it instead of being burned.

In Devon, the seventeen of us living in the villa in Dittisham were the first rank of Andrew's students. Other, newer students looked up to us, tried to get our attention, tried to get invited to our house. Now, in Amherst, there are about ten student houses, and there is a kind of hierarchy which seems clear. Andrew's house is of course the first, with Andrew, Alka, and a handful of intimate students. In the second house, which is near Andrew's, live students who often cook for Andrew, and whom Andrew often visits. Our house is the third in rank. The ranking of a house is determined by the degree to which Andrew's teachings are being lived. To keep us focused we begin to have regular house meetings in which we evaluate how well we are living the teachings. The problem is there are no clear guidelines for that, only unwritten ones. One of Andrew's main points is that you don't have to do anything to be free; you don't have to meditate, pray, perform rituals or do other spiritual practices. We are already free, and we only have to stay aware of that. But then what does it mean in day-to-day reality to be free? There's only a negative definition of that: if we behave in an egocentric way, cut ourselves off, want to protect our privacy, hold on to special relationships, then we are not free. Or, it means we resist the fact that we are always already free because we want to hold on to our separate ego. So to keep a standard we have to take a firm stand with each other if we notice such resistance.

2.2. The House Meeting

We're all sitting in the living room facing each other. Dinner and coffee are finished, and it is time for our house meeting. There is an uncomfortable silence. There are eight of us. I sit in the chair near the front window. On a couch next to me are Lucy and Jean, two English women in their thirties. On the chair opposite me is Luna,

Andrew's mother. Over the past weeks I've grown very fond of her. She's psychologically astute, and unafraid to be critical of Andrew and the community. After Andrew's miraculous meeting with Poonjaji, Luna was one of the first people he'd called. Ecstatic about the transformation he'd experienced, he told her to take the first plane to India. And she had done so, becoming one of his first students. Now, after having been with her son in Rishikesh, she's moved out of her apartment in New York City to join us in Amherst. Sarah is sitting in the chair between Luna and me.

Lucy starts to speak. "I want to bring something up that I've been noticing," she says, "having to do with how Andre and Sarah are relating to each other."

I freeze. Is there anything wrong with our relationship? Sarah and I are the only two in the house in a sexual relationship, and Andrew has been speaking in satsang these days about the attachment in sexual relationships, and how the romantic illusion can lead us away from enlightenment because we get infatuated. I remember the couple from Boston that Andrew has been speaking to about this—they've decided to split up for six months to investigate their attachment to each other. Lucy has also recently split up from her husband Rudy. She lives with her two sons in our house, while he lives in another student house.

She continues, "You know how Andrew has been speaking about no personal attachments, about the importance of not holding on to our fixed relationships just out of habit and conditioning. I've noticed how there is something sticky in the way that you relate to each other. You give each other special looks, and special attention. I feel, Andre, that you are spending more time with Sarah than with the other people in the house." Other people nod in agreement. Obviously, this point has been discussed prior to the house meeting.

I shift uncomfortably in my seat. My first impulse is to rebel, to jump out of my chair and tell them that I don't agree, that they should mind their own business. But that's my ego speaking of course, wanting to protect my private life. It doesn't want to investigate honestly and without prejudice, doesn't want to consider that maybe Sarah and I are too attached to each other. But I have to admit to myself that I don't fully trust Lucy's motives for speaking out against Sarah and me. I know she and Sarah don't get along very well. And maybe she's taking it out on us because she had to split from her husband.

But this is all personal, secondary stuff. The main thing is to look at this from the standpoint of Andrew's teaching. That's what we're trying to do in these house meetings. And I recognize that what Lucy is saying is exactly the point Andrew has been speaking about. Sarah and I are spending more time together than with the others. I find that difficult to give up; in a certain way it simply feels natural to me for us to spend more time together. We're in a relationship after all. But this stickiness is a personal conditioning that we are both holding on to. To give up this personal attachment is the sacrifice that Andrew is asking from us. So I say to Lucy that she has a point, and that this is something that Sarah and I have to look into. The others question me about how serious I am about changing this pattern, and after a bit of talking they seem convinced by my sincerity.

Now the conversation turns to Sarah. Jean, a fairly dominant woman with glasses and middle-length red hair, talks about a conversation that we had a few days ago. During that conversation Sarah had said with a happy smile that she and I had had sex every night for the past week. Jean now throws that in to prove that Sarah is indulging in her sexual desires, that she is not living the teachings, that she is throwing away her freedom by taking refuge in her attachment to me. Other people agree. I keep silent. I feel it's hardly appropriate for me to say anything about this. But I don't like the way Jean is going about it. I feel she's exaggerating. But then, my judgment is probably clouded because of my attachment to Sarah. Maybe this is exactly a sign of how attached we are.

Sarah is now questioned more deeply by several of us, and she's becoming more and more upset. She starts crying. Lucy tells her not to try to escape facing the truth by pretending to be emotional and weak. And so the meeting goes from bad to worse. It feels terrible to see Sarah under the gun, but at the same time I feel she has to look into this. She has to take a stand with this emotional weakness, for the sake of her own liberation. But the others in the house don't feel Sarah is doing this now. They tell her she is being evasive, defensive, emotional, and sentimental. At the end of the meeting everyone is quiet. Sarah has not 'come through'. Coming through would have meant that she not only agreed with the criticisms, but would have also apologized in an emotionally convincing way, and have shown to the others that she was genuinely abhorred with the behavior that had just been exposed. She is unwilling to face herself in this way. Instead, she has just fallen apart—buckled under the pressure. This is not a good sign. It pains me to see her like this.

As we go to bed Sarah apologizes to me, tells me that she will make herself stronger. I try to reassure her that everything will be all right. I tell her it's good that we let go of our attachment to each other; that this is why we are here with Andrew. She nods. I hope that she will come through but I'm not sure about it.

The next day there is a lot of talk about our house meeting the day before. Andrew has been briefed, and he wants this sorted out to the bottom. I go for a walk with Luna. She is very outspoken. She feels that Lucy and Jean were on a power trip. I hesitate. I tell her that I had similar suspicions but that I can hardly be expected to be objective.

"Nonsense, you should have said something," she says in her usual direct way, "let's call another meeting."

So that evening there is another house meeting. Luna speaks out about her misgivings with Lucy and Jean. Lucy and Jean argue with her. They say she is too psychological, too intellectual. I try to keep the peace and steer a middle course. Then Sarah herself begins to speak. She agrees with everything that Lucy and Jean have said. Sobbing loudly, she berates herself for being so weak and sentimental. I don't know what to say. I feel angry at Lucy and Jean for making Sarah go to pieces like this, but at the same time I can see that Sarah is clinging to me. Maybe everyone's right. Maybe she would grow up more if she were forced to stand on her own two feet. Would it be better for us to separate? Should we sleep in separate rooms for a while? I find it hard to put aside my personal feelings for Sarah and stand by the larger, objective truth of the situation. But that is exactly what Andrew is asking us to do.

The situation with Sarah continues for what seems an eternity but is probably about a week. In satsang Andrew speaks again against the insidious attachments of romantic relationships. Then Sarah makes a panic-stricken move. Without talking to me, she tells Jean and Lucy that she is breaking up with me. Is this a heroic deed in service of the revolution, or a desperate measure to placate her attackers? Jean and Lucy are satisfied with Sarah's sudden move, but I feel hurt because Sarah hasn't told me anything. Even though I've seen other couples in the community split up, I am taken aback now that it is our turn. Everyone consoles me and tells me that this is the price we have to pay for liberation. They compliment me for the firm stand I've taken in all this. But I have a feeling that I should have done more to stand up for Sarah. Was this the best way to deal with the whole situation? Is this bringing us any closer to enlightenment?

"I understand it's very tough for you now," Harry says. "But really, this is all for the best. We're in the midst of a revolution, you know, and that revolution is asking a big price from all of us."

"Yes, but what does it have to do with enlightenment, for God's sake?"

"Well, you know that enlightenment is not just a blissful state of surrender, some kind of bubble to spend the rest of our lives in. Enlightenment demands personal change from each of us. We have to take responsibility for our conditioning, our shortcomings, our selfishness, and attachments. After realizing the secret of enlightenment, our behavior should express that realization perfectly, that's the whole point. That's what is so revolutionary about what Andrew's trying to do."

"Yes, but should we be so ruthless with each other?"

"I understand that you feel bad about what happened, but that's the price we have to pay. The challenge is to do it with passion, with determination and an absolute commitment. That's what we need to pull it off. But look at how amazing this all is! This is an evolutionary experiment; we are the forerunners in an evolutionary wave that will transform the western spiritual world!"

The whole drama has obviously not gone unnoticed in the community. Andrew has been kept informed all along. He calls Sarah and me to his room after satsang. He is upset with Sarah because of the way she has ended the relationship. He tells her it's like sticking a knife in my back. I think back to my conversation with Andrew in Devon. Was he right after all to be cautious about Sarah and I being in a relationship?

Sarah moves into another house, and for about a year we hardly have any contact. After that our relationship becomes more normal, like any two community members.

This is my first personal experience of the price that has to be paid for liberation. Now I've felt first-hand that

Andrew means business when he says that clarity of intention is all-important, and that we have to be completely responsible for the choices we make. Taking a stand with Sarah, allowing the relationship to end has been my first real sacrifice for the revolution.

Everyone in the community praises me for my dedication to the teachings, and my willingness to make this sacrifice, to cut deeply into my own attachments for the sake of enlightenment. I had to make a choice between my attachment to Sarah, and the demands of enlightenment. I chose for the demands of enlightenment, and therefore against the feelings in my own heart for Sarah. From a human point of view it's been painful, but from a larger perspective I've chosen wisely, they say.

2.3. Boston

Throughout the summer of 1988, more people from Europe arrive in Amherst. Nearly all of them have come to stay. They have finished up their business in Europe, sold their houses, quit their jobs, and taken their children from school. There are new American arrivals as well. Among them are four ex-disciples of another American guru. They live in Boston and travel one and a half hours each way to come to satsang in Amherst every day. But to our deep regret, the American Buddhists don't come. One of the reasons appears to be that people are spreading tales about Andrew, saying there is a dark side to him, and that Andrew has a problem with power and authority. We're outraged about such accusations. The four Boston students invite Andrew to come and teach in Boston.

Andrew accepts. This means relocation for most of us. Hopefully Boston will attract more spiritually interested people.

Up until now we've lived together in an idyllic paradise as if money didn't exist. Most of us had some savings, some people had borrowed money, a few lucky ones like Harry were financially independent. Andrew himself lives on a small yearly inheritance. But now most of us have to start looking for work. We take jobs that allow us to make good money while working a minimal number of hours. Most of us do house cleaning or window washing. I manage to find a job as a Dutch translator and computer consultant, which also gives me a working permit. Andrew teaches five nights a week in the local Montessori school. They are public teachings now, not living room gatherings as before. In the cold Boston winter we line up for forty-five minutes outside to get a good seat. Andrew sits on a podium, surrounded by exuberant bouquets of flowers. It has become customary to accompany letters to Andrew with flowers: as an expression of love, an apology after a faux pas, or to thank him for his wonderful teachings. The local florist becomes a good friend of many community members.

Although community life is more structured now and there is less time to simply hang out together, we still have great community parties. Everyone dances the whole night long. There are no distracting sexual vibes, just an ecstatic celebration of intimacy. There's no alcohol served, but we don't need alcohol to get intoxicated.

In Boston the house meetings become ever more central. It's not the experience of oneness that is important (that is now a given), but whether our lives are an expression of what we have realized. More and more often people are being sent out of houses when they don't meet the standard. My own house falls apart after a few months because of irreconcilable differences between people. Andrew is angry with me because he feels I've been too passive, and have been trying for too long to keep the peace instead of confronting people and taking a stand. He calls me a wimp. Andrew often uses such strong language in order to shock the ego. I agree with him that this is just my ego shrinking back from standing up for the truth. I feel ashamed to have disappointed him. I call his house to speak to him, but he doesn't want to talk. I feel I've blown it. I have to move to another house. I apply for several houses but am rejected because now my track record is not good. Eventually I find a spot in a lower ranking house. To my surprise I discover that I'm actually much happier in this lower house, and start to make real friendships with the people there.

2.4. Luna's Defection

Andrew stays in Boston until April 1989, but the community doesn't grow substantially. Apparently the East Coast is not receptive to Andrew's message, and Andrew decides to move to the Mecca of spirituality, Marin County in California. The entire community of one hundred and fifty people, still mostly Europeans, drives across the country to set up shop in Marin, to find housing and jobs.

I drive cross country with five others in two weeks. We drive in two cars from Boston to Virginia, Nashville, Memphis (where we visit Elvis' house Graceland), the Grand Canyon, Las Vegas, Yosemite, to arrive in the San Francisco Bay Area. We have a great time.

By July we're all assembled in Northern California, waiting for Andrew, who is still in Boston, to come. But then an unexpected event: Andrew's mother Luna leaves. I know that over the past few months she has grown increasingly ambivalent about what she calls Andrew's whole guru setup. As a result Andrew has given her an increasingly hard time about her lack of surrender and her cynicism. Now the shocking news comes that Luna has left the community together with four other students after meeting the Indian anti-guru U.G. Krishnamurti, who's renowned for debunking gurus and "the whole enlightenment business" as he calls it. Luna now flatly disagrees with what happens in the student houses. She feels Andrew's vision has deteriorated into a kind of fascism, where everyone lives in fear of punishment. U.G. has convinced her that there is no such thing as enlightenment, and that every guru, including Andrew, is only out to manipulate his students and control them.

The news about Luna's defection is unexpected and shocking to me. I am torn in my loyalties, not only because of my friendship with Luna, but also because of my former memories of U.G. In 1983, when I was in Saanen to listen to Jiddu Krishnamurti who gave talks there every summer, I had heard about "the second Krishnamurti" who lived in Gstaad next to Saanen. I was fascinated. The story went that U.G. (no relation to J.) had been raised to become a great spiritual teacher, that he had rejected the whole enlightenment business and had for years lived as a street bum. Somehow he had undergone some kind of transformation, almost in spite of himself, but he was strongly opposed to gurus. He claimed the whole enlightenment business was nonsense. That's why he was called the anti-guru guru. I took a walk through the mountains right up to his porch. There he sat in his garden and invited me in. He seemed absolutely unsurprised to see me turn up like that. We talked for half an hour about meditation, spiritual practice, and enlightenment, and then I was on my way. Since that time I had been a fan of U.G.

Andrew, still in Boston, is furious. A community meeting is set up where Luna is declared a persona non grata. I find it impossible to understand why Luna has left Andrew in such a bitter way. Of course there are shortcomings in the community, but in all revolutionary movements there are mistakes made and things to be learned. I know she must still love Andrew. She shouldn't listen to the objections of her mind. I try to phone her to tell her that, but she doesn't want to speak to anyone from the community. I am sad to see her leave. I write her a letter: how could she hurt her beloved son and Master so much? A few weeks later Luna sends me a short note in return. The community has become a fascist organization, she reiterates, and everyone lives in fear of Andrew. She doesn't want to have anything to do with it anymore. I have lost her as a friend, but there is nothing I can do. I tell Andrew about Luna's note to me, and he says he is also deeply unhappy about how his own mother has turned against him. He's happy that I've written to Luna and that I stand by him in these difficult times.

2.5. Birth of a Formal Sangha

In the summer of 1989, satsang starts in Marin, in the Corte Madera yoga center. Marin is a focal point of spirituality, like Totnes in Devon, home to a large number of spiritual seekers, meditation teachers, gurus, psychics, healers and therapists. Andrew, by now, has a reputation of being a controversial spiritual teacher who is out to shake up the contemporary spiritual scene. His message of enlightenment here and now is heresy for some of the western Buddhist meditation teachers who advocate spiritual practice and gradual improvement over time. His renunciate stance based on clarity of intention goes against the prevailing views of many transpersonal psychologists who say you have to integrate enlightenment into your personal life rather than giving your life over to enlightenment as Andrew says. So when Andrew starts satsang, quite a few of the local experts come to check him out. They like Andrew, they like the blissful experiences that satsang gives them, but they don't like us, Andrew's hundred and fifty, mostly European, students, that silently attend satsang, adoring our spiritual Master, writing him love letters. The Californians, used to an individualized and sophisticated lifestyle, are turned off by this European crowd of neo-hippies, who are content to clean houses for a living, live in groups of ten in three-bedroom houses, don't mind a life without privacy, and generally seem like rather simplistic followers. They feel we behave like sheep. "Androids," they call us.

We don't mind. Life in Marin is still mostly paradise. There's beautiful scenery all around. On the weekends we go to beautiful beaches or for long walks on Mount Tamalpais. We're one big spiritual family on a continuous high. Four nights a week we go to satsang and spend a long time afterwards speaking about Andrew's talks, his profound dialogs with people. We work two or three days a week, just enough to support ourselves, and for the rest of the time we hang out together.

* * *

There's a hushed silence in the Corte Madera yoga center. A hundred and fifty of us are sitting cross-legged in a U-shape around a platform decorated with flowers, waiting for Andrew to arrive. Another twenty people or so, mostly newcomers, are sitting on chairs in the back. There's a sense of anticipation in the room. The doors open and Andrew walks in. He's dressed in smart black pants and a gorgeously colorful short-sleeve shirt with elaborate patterns, no doubt a gift from one of us. He sits down and closes his eyes. We sit in silence together for about twenty minutes. Then Andrew starts to speak. He welcomes everybody and asks if there are any questions.

A middle-aged woman raises her hand. I know her. She's been around the block in the spiritual scene, has visited many teachers and meditated for many years.

"The Buddha spoke about the importance of sangha, of spiritual community. Can you say more about how you see that? Is being part of a sangha necessary for getting enlightened?"

Andrew sits still for a few moments before he responds.

"A sangha is a community of finders, of people who've had a profound awakening experience. A sangha is a group of people who have come together only because they want to give themselves utterly to being free. In that complete giving they are committed to overcome anything that could ever interfere with the perfect expression of perfect enlightenment and perfect liberation. That's the meaning of sangha."

Andrew pauses briefly and takes a sip from the glass of water on the side table next to his chair.

"That's a great answer," I think. "He's destroying her fixed ideas that a sangha is about getting something. A community of finders, yes, that sums up my experience. We're not out to get anything anymore, we're just enjoying each other's company and our living together in our new found freedom."

Andrew continues, "When fellow finders come together, they share the end of seeking and the end of waiting. When you come to the end of seeking and the end of waiting, something changes inside, the chemistry changes. Tremendous joy and deep trust in life itself is realized when you've truly found what you've been looking for."

The woman is still not quite convinced. She asks, "Why would people choose to come together in this way?"

Andrew smiles in his usual disarming and charming way.

"Well, for no other reason than the joy of it, the ecstasy of it, and because it's precious to be in a situation where there wouldn't be any hindrance to the perfect spontaneity of being truly awake."

* * *

No hindrance to the perfect spontaneity of being truly awake — this sentence sticks in my mind the next few days. It sounds great, but what does it mean practically?

Well, for one thing it means having our house meetings, pointing out to each other that we have to change even at the risk of being asked to leave our house if we prove unwilling to change. It's all part of the process of spiritual transformation.

But Andrew now takes things a step further. He calls us together for a community meeting, and explains to us that things will be different from now on. He wants our living according to the standard of enlightenment to be visible to the outside world. He formalizes the community of the more dedicated students and calls it 'the Sangha' (a Buddhist term for the community of monks and nuns). Other people, such as visitors from Europe, or those who have not made a formal commitment to the teachings are called lay students. He tells the men and the women of the Sangha to meet in separate meetings (men with men, women with women) twice a week to discuss his teachings and to increase the standard to which we are living them, just as we have been doing in the house meetings. The full Sangha also now has private meetings where "Sangha business," meaning internal community affairs, is handled. A strict separation is introduced between "family business" and public affairs. The men's and women's meetings soon take over the previous function of the house meetings.

* * *

Coming home from work one day I notice there's a frantic excitement in our apartment. Two of my five housemates greet me at the door. "Come in quick," they say, "Andrew has come over for a surprise visit. The others are already in the jacuzzi with him."

I quickly change my clothes and hurry with the others to the jacuzzi in our apartment complex. We let ourselves down into the hot and bubbling water. There are no other people around except for Andrew and the five of us. First we sit together in blissful silence. The sun is still warm at this time of day.

Soon we become engaged in frantic conversation. Andrew starts talking about Juliette, one of our fellow students. He's not happy with her. She's a vivacious and attractive French woman who joined us in Devon. She has a reputation for being flirtatious. Andrew says she's struggling with her ego, stuck in her conditioning of being an attractive woman who is getting affirmation by attention from men. We're all right there with Andrew, and agree with him.

"I see what you mean," says one of my housemates, "It's outrageous how stubborn she is, she just won't change this thing."

"Yes, she's a baby," says Andrew.

"A baby and very weak," my housemate confirms. We all laugh. But for one brief moment there's a sudden gush of fear inside me. What if it's me next time that everyone is talking about?

The situation with Juliette doesn't improve. Andrew feels it's time for stronger measures. Juliette walks into satsang one evening with her head completely shaved. It's a jarring sight. We hear that Andrew has told her to be celibate, and to shave her head in the same way that renunciate monks in the eastern traditions do. It's meant as a kind of shock therapy to cure her of her endless fascination with herself, her appearance, and with men. It isn't long before others are to follow. Soon, there are about eight students who are bald and celibate, and Andrew tells them to live together in the same house. Once every two weeks they have a meeting where they shave each other's heads and discuss renunciation and celibacy.

(Eventually about one fifth of the community becomes shaven celibates. Although from the outside this often seems unsettling, even disturbing, particularly for new people visiting the community, I hear from many of the celibates themselves that they feel it is a great learning experience. Living together with male and female celibates provides an opportunity to escape fixed gender roles. There is an equality and intimacy between men and women in a way that is hardly known in the world.)

* * *

Graham is one of the students who had invited Andrew to teach in Boston. He was used to quite a materialistic lifestyle before meeting Andrew, and a last remnant of this is a beautiful Saab. He is notorious for his attachment to his Saab. In Boston Andrew had already pressed him to sell the car. Graham promised to do so, but kept postponing it. Now Andrew presses him to sell it a second and third time. But again Graham hesitates and tries to renegotiate. He desperately wants to keep the car. It gradually turns into a battle of wills: Andrew is battling Graham's ego, trying to wrestle his attachment away from him. We speak with Graham in the men's meeting, trying to get him to give up his attachment to his car and everything that it stands for. But although Graham says he's on our side, we feel he doesn't really want to let go. As the drama continues, the pressure mounts. In the end Andrew radicalizes the situation, just as he did with Juliette. The standard of enlightenment is black or white, so if it isn't white, it will be black. Andrew calls Graham and tells him he's going to solve the dilemma for him once and for all. He will go with Graham to the junkyard and have the Saab crushed. After his initial responses of disbelief, panic, rage and desperation, Graham eventually agrees. We all hold our breath collectively. We can't believe it. A $20,000 car is going to be destroyed for the sake of Graham's spiritual evolution. It's the ultimate act of renunciation, like in the classical stories of the scholar who threw his beloved books into the Ganges or the Buddha who left his wife and child behind.

In satsang the next evening Andrew tells the whole story to a disbelieving crowd. Graham and Andrew went to the junkyard with the Saab. The operator there initially refused to crush the car, thinking he was dealing with a pair of nutcases. But Andrew and Graham insisted. To maximize the effect Andrew had Graham push the button that turned the car into pulp. Andrew says it was a momentous cleansing ritual, a powerful boost for Graham. He points to Graham, who indeed seems to have undergone some kind of transformation. He's beaming with self-confidence because he has taken such a firm stance against his ego. We're in awe. Andrew had the guts to take this to the extreme, and he was right—look at Graham sitting there beaming! So this is what it takes to do battle with the ego.

2.6. 'Going For It' in the Men's Meetings

Two times a week now the men's meetings take place, where we speak together about the teachings, about what it is to lead a spiritual life. The meetings are a testing ground for our clarity about the teachings, our perceptions about each other, our courage, our willingness to expose ourselves and the parts that we are not so proud of and would rather hide. It is exciting and sometimes daunting to venture into unknown territory together like this, to have no secrets from each other, to be completely trusting and intimate, to find out what we are made of. Some of us are resistant and argue, and some become completely paralyzed when they find themselves in the light of collective scrutiny.

In the beginning I tend to be fairly quiet and shy in the meetings. Then Andrew sends me a message, he wants me to get completely involved, to be out there. He says I'm not really 'going for it'. 'Going for it' is one of these Sangha expressions that has taken on a life of its own. It means energetically and fearlessly applying yourself to the teachings, and making sure that others are too. After all, we're in this together.

* * *

Its 8 p.m. Forty men sit cross-legged on meditation cushions in a large circle in the living room of one of the Sangha houses. A silence hangs in the room. We all look at each other's faces, unsure who will kick off this men's meeting. Then a timid voice pipes up, "I'd like to speak tonight." We turn to look at Rudy, a tall blond Englishman whom we all like. Since he split up with Lucy last year he's been doing great, but recently he's been a bit more distant. It makes sense to us that he wants to speak tonight. Andrew had called him yesterday, and had said to him that he gives too little of himself within the community, and keeps himself too much in the background. It's good that Rudy wants to investigate this.

As Rudy is telling us what's going on for him, it becomes clear that he is still harboring all kinds of worldly desires. Hesitantly he confesses that at his job he feels attracted to a woman. A long discussion ensues.

"Now it makes sense why we feel that you're holding back from the other people in our house," one of Rudy's housemates says. "You're not really present. You seem more interested in your work, that woman and your career than in being with us."

"No, that's not true," Rudy says. He nervously shifts his legs. "I know I've felt tempted to go back into the world, but that's not what I really want. I want to be with all of you. That's where my heart really is."

"But Rudy," John says with a stern expression, "we hear you say that, but we don't feel it." Other men nod in agreement. "We don't feel it in our guts that you really want to be with us. You feel very distant."

John is an American and is Andrew's top student. He and Robert, an English ex-Buddhist, often take the lead in our meetings. They're also the ones who keep Andrew informed.

Little droplets of sweat start to appear on Rudy's forehead. He can't seem to keep his hands still.

"It's really true guys. I feel very close to all of you. You mean everything to me." His voice is just a notch too high.

John says, "I would love to believe you Rudy, but I'm just not convinced. It feels to me that this woman at your work has a bigger place in your heart than all of us."

Now Rudy raises his voice. "I really mean it guys, my heart is with you."

"Well, you have to find a way to prove it to us," Robert says, "because none of us is actually convinced."

Silence. The tension in the room is mounting. I shift uncomfortably on my cushion. Rudy seems about to collapse. He looks at the floor and seems completely paralyzed. Five long minutes go by.

"Rudy, what's happening?" John says, "I feel we're losing you. You can't run away from us like that. You're jerking us around. It's pretty disgusting actually."

I feel a knot in my stomach. It's so tense in the room. I can only guess at what Rudy feels this moment.

Then suddenly Rudy looks up, his face contorted. "I love you!" he shouts at the top of his voice. It's embarrassing. We don't know what to say or do.

It's Robert who takes the lead. "Don't be so unreal, Rudy. You're wasting our time."

The meeting goes on hour after hour. Rudy apologizes, promises to change his ways, and tells us how much he wants to be with us. But we are not convinced he means it. Thirty-nine men try to bring Rudy to reason. At five a.m. we end the meeting. No one is convinced that Rudy is truly prepared to let go of his worldly desires or that he wants to.

When Andrew hears about this meeting he is livid. He sends Rudy a message in which he condemns him and insults him. He sends him away from the Sangha. We are stunned. This is not what we expected. But Andrew means business. Over the next weeks, more men and women are sent away from the Sangha. They mostly continue to live in the area, as lay students. By December 1989, only eighty of the initial 120 students are left in the formal Sangha. I find all this hard to stomach, but this is the price we have to pay to practice a teaching as radical as Andrew's.

* * *

The living room in Mill Valley is crammed with people. Eighty of us are packed together listening to Andrew. He has called this meeting with the Sangha to speak about how things are going, and the fact that so many people are leaving.

"I can understand that many of you are feeling shaky and confused," he says, "but I'm convinced that this is the only way. Many people say they want to be enlightened, but very few people actually want to change, because change can be difficult and painful, and can require big sacrifices. A spiritual community should be a place where people who aren't serious about their own evolution wouldn't be able to survive. It should be far more challenging than living in the normal world where there is no standard, and where compromise is very acceptable. A true Sangha is a proving ground, a constant testing, where everyone finds out how serious they are."

From my seat in the back of the room I let this sink in. This is a different image of Sangha than a joyous community of finders. Those happy, innocent days seem to be behind us. The Sangha now sounds more like a spiritual boot camp.

A woman raises her hand and asks, "What about how harsh we are with the people that are falling short? Shouldn't we be more supportive, accepting and loving each other unconditionally so we can help each other to grow?"

Andrew looks shocked for a moment, as if he can't believe she's actually asked this question. Then, with a slightly raised voice, he says, "Have you been listening to my teaching at all? You sound like one of these new age freaks that speak about loving yourself and nurturing the inner child. You know how I feel about that?" Andrew slits a hand across his throat and laughs, a strange cackling laugh that we've all gotten used to.

"I don't like unconditional love," he says. "Love always has to be earned."

I nod. I used to believe that Andrew loved me no matter what, but now I know that I have to be worthy of his love. I have to stand at his side in his revolution, then we can share in an impersonal love. I feel full of fire and determination to carry the banner of enlightenment, like the knights of King Arthur looking for the Holy Grail, but at the same time I miss the old days where I could just be a 'finder'.

Andrew looks more relaxed now and drinks are being passed around. We talk more personally and intimately together. Andrew shares with us what it's like for him being a spiritual teacher.

"You know, in the beginning I still felt I had some private life outside being a teacher, but now I've come to accept that my role as a teacher will always completely consume me. I've always said that if enlightenment is truly more important to you than anything else, you have to be willing to make big sacrifices for it."

I feel for Andrew. I think about his mother leaving; what a sacrifice he's making for the sake of enlightenment. He truly has no personal life left. I feel guilty and small-minded for my own complaints about the sacrifices I have to make. How minor and unimportant they seem compared to what Andrew is giving up. Of course it's painful to see some of our comrades fall or get wounded, but that's to be expected in a battle of this kind, a battle against the ego.

2.7. The Book

During our stay in Boston Andrew was working on a book about his miraculous meeting with Poonja and his transformation as a result of it. A few intimi were allowed to work with him on it. In May 1989, it was published under the title *My Master Is My Self*. Now Andrew is working on a second book, which is not about his life, but about his teachings of enlightenment. He wants it to be his magnum opus, the book that will shake the spiritual world by its depth and power. The book will be based on the transcriptions of his satsangs. Every satsang is recorded and typed out verbatim by a group of Andrew's closest students. It is an enviable job. In September 1989, I put in an application to be allowed to transcribe. Even though English is not my native language I am accepted. I am thrilled.

Two weeks later it gets even better. Andrew calls me. This is now a rare occurrence, since mostly someone from the community office calls on his behalf. After a few minutes of small talk he asks me if I want to work on his new book with John. I am overjoyed. I feel like I've won the lottery. I tell him, yes, of course I want to. I'd love to. "Okay, speak to John about it then, but don't let me down." I hasten to assure him that I won't betray the trust he is putting in me. I am over the moon with such an honorable assignment. Work with John! Like everyone I look up to him immensely. He is Andrew's right hand man. He is the same age as me, 26, and has also studied philosophy. I haven't had much personal contact with him so far, because he is so much closer to Andrew. I am very happy to serve Andrew and the teachings in such an important way. Overjoyed, I write a thank you letter to Andrew that I deliver to his place with a big bunch of flowers.

Over the next couple of months John gives me thick files full of transcripts of Andrew's satsangs, from 1986 to 1989. In the early days John scribbled down some notes in satsang, but these days every evening is taped, and the best dialogs and teachings are transcribed verbatim. The three hundred satsangs that have been transcribed so far form a body of material about four thousand pages in length. John and I read everything, and give each dialog a valuation from one to five, five being the highest. I record everything in a database on the computer. The ones and the twos we discard. By the beginning of November we have two thousand pages left. Now the next round of selecting and discarding starts. Long dialogs we reduce to their essence, and the threes are discarded. A complicating factor is that new transcripts continue to come in and almost always seem to be better than the material that we have read so far.

* * *

Slowly I steer my car around the many curves of the hill in Larkspur. I'm on my way to a meeting with John about the book, not at the office, our usual meeting place, but at Andrew's house, where John also lives. Looking out at the road I am reminded of Matt, an English student, who last month prostrated the entire way up this road to Andrew's house in order to convince Andrew that he was serious in wanting to take on his ego. As I come nearer the top of the hill, a sense of excitement and nervousness comes over me. It's great to have close personal contact with Andrew, but on the other hand any wrong gesture, any wrong word, any tension, can reveal parts of my ego that Andrew will pick up on.

I ring the doorbell and Andrew opens the door. He's in a training suit, and yawning, he invites me in. Probably he's just done yoga. The house looks immaculately clean, with flowers everywhere. As I take off my shoes I peek at the notice board on the wall, where he puts up the best letters he receives each week. I am overjoyed to see my own letter hanging there, a note consisting of just one word, a big YES splattered all over the page.

In the living room we sit down. Andrew tells John to make cappuccino, and teases him non-stop while he's doing it. John seems to be used to it. It feels great to be hanging out with Andrew like this. He feels like just a regular American guy, so human and accessible. Yes, I'm definitely in love with this guy.

"So what do you think of Matt?" Andrew asks me. I feel honored that he asks my opinion.

"I think he showed his seriousness," I answer, referring to Matt's prostration exercise.

"Do you hear that?" Andrew calls out to John in the kitchen, "Andre thinks that Matt has shown his seriousness. How can you work with a wimp like that?" And to me he says, "Matt's not serious at all. He's a very aggressive guy. This prostration thing is all a big performance." He yawns again and says, "I've been thinking to send him to Thailand for a year."

Matt had been a Buddhist monk for many years before meeting Andrew. I swallow. I'm not used to people's lives being decided in such seemingly casual ways.

John brings in the coffee and the talk continues about Ken Wilber, a well-known author in spiritual circles. When Andrew stayed for the month in my Amsterdam apartment, he had seen my bookcase stacked with Ken

Wilber books, since I'd done my psychology thesis on him. Andrew had picked up one of them, and had been very impressed. Since that time Andrew has been eager to get him as a student, and we brainstorm about how we can pull him in. We speculate about why he hasn't been willing to meet with Andrew. Is he afraid of ego death?

"Wait until he reads your book," I say. "He will be haunted by the absoluteness of your teachings." Andrew likes that.

"Okay guys," he calls out, "then back to work on it. The sooner it comes out, the better. It's gonna be great!"

"Yes!" John and I call out, "it's gonna be great!"

* * *

John and I continue to wade through an almost inexhaustible pile of material, make a thematic chapter structure, and arrive late December at a selection of five hundred pages. The best of the best. The past months we have often been spending long hours deep into the night in a small basement office, reading and rating one dialog after another. It's been great to go through all this material, but it's also starting to take its toll. John is exhausted and I'm not in much better shape. Andrew is in England for the month and will be back in a week. John and I are planning to have a draft version of the book ready for him when he comes back. We can't wait to show our material to Andrew.

2.8. Gina: The Prelude

Gina arrives in California, fresh from London, in July 1989. She's a 37-year-old Greek woman with a strong passion for enlightenment. She has traveled to India and has spent time with the renowned Nisargadatta. She moves into the Dawn Court house, where I live as well. We were six in the house, but within months of her arrival there are only three of us left.

My star is rising now within the community. My work on Andrew's book puts me high up in the ranking. I am confident in the men's meetings, speaking with clarity and conviction about Andrew's teachings. Everybody feels I am taking a firm stand. Andrew is happy with me. Nothing could possibly be better. I feel wonderful and self assured, and the one person in my house to share this with is Gina. Often we stay up at night and have moving conversations about Andrew's teachings. When we look into each other's eyes we feel a deep intimacy.

For Gina it all seems to be purely platonic. But I start to suspect something has changed when she goes to the hairdresser for a special cut, and seems quite interested in whether I like it. Any ambiguity seems to be resolved during one of our nightly conversations when she suddenly grabs my hand and looks at me in a penetrating way.

"Andre, I've never felt with a man what I'm feeling with you."

She says it quietly, but the underlying intensity is palpable. I want to jump into bed with her on the spot. I meet her intense gaze and say, "I feel the same way."

We continue to sit like that for a while, then we get up. I make a clumsy attempt to embrace her, but she is not into it. For a moment she has almost lost control over herself, but now she has regained it.

"Good night, Andre," she says.

The next day, when we are alone together in the house, we talk about the amazing intimacy that we have experienced.

"It was as if the Absolute was directly manifesting itself through us," Gina says. I think it better not to mention that I have experienced things in a slightly more earthy way. Then we look each other deep in the eyes and sit there for a while. I feel the intensity grow between us. There it is again, that unbearably close feeling. And again my lower instincts respond, but now with such force that I ejaculate on the spot. What just happened? Was this the Absolute manifesting through us, as Gina feels? The thought, God works in mysterious ways, flashes through me. Gina seems completely absorbed by our gazes holding each other. She looks perfectly happy.

Although largely unspoken, there is an underlying puritanical attitude toward sexuality in the community. So this tastes like forbidden fruit. I talk with no one about my experience. I feel guilty. Such an indulgence in sexual titillation is not exactly in line with the teachings. What would they all think of me if they knew about this? I find it hard to admit even to myself that I'm falling in love. Deep down I still harbor the memory of my relationship with Sarah — I don't want to go through anything like that again. Gina and I go for a walk together to talk about what is developing between us. I am aware of my intense sexual attraction to her, but she is talking in terms of a noble meeting of souls, a meeting in spirit. We speak about the possibility of getting into a relationship, but no, that would be impossible, we both feel. How can we put a personal, sexual relationship before enlightenment? Gina wholeheartedly agrees, but I suspect she may be having a hard time with her own feelings, that perhaps she can't admit to herself that they are of a sexual nature. In satsang she has a few strange interactions with Andrew that reveal a certain intensity which everyone wonders about. She seems to become more and more confused. She is spoken to in the women's meetings, things go from bad to worse, and eventually she has to leave the house in Marin Court. After she leaves, the downward spiral continues. A few months later things have gone so bad for her that she decides to leave the Sangha and move back to London. From the airport Gina calls me to say goodbye. I feel sorry for her, but I'm also learning now to steel myself off from my personal feelings. It's too painful to let in the human drama.

3

FACE EVERYTHING AND AVOID NOTHING

If we want to be free more than anything else, we have to be willing to face everything and avoid nothing in every moment.

-Andrew Cohen

3.1. Lunatic

It's January 1990. John calls me. He has to take care that Andrew's house is in tiptop shape when Andrew comes back next week. He has to shop and clean. "Can you prepare the draft of the book for Andrew?" he asks.

I'm not sure how I can ever manage that by myself but I say, "Yes, sure, just leave it to me."

Like a madman I go to work. All the dialogs have to be brought into the same format on the computer and then printed; some handwritten dialogs must be typed up. It's an enormous job. I work late into the nights, and when Andrew comes back John and I proudly show him the first draft of Enlightenment is a Secret. Under its shiny exterior, this draft still contains many small errors, omissions, and sloppy mistakes – something I would have done better to be very clear about.

Andrew asks Robert to help out. I have mixed feelings about that. The more help the better of course but I feel pushed aside. John lives with Andrew and Robert is over at Andrew's house every day. I don't belong to their inner circle but I'm tolerated because I work on the book. At least that's how it feels to me.

The sessions with Andrew start. We're sitting on the floor in his living room. John, Robert and I read the dialogs we like best out aloud. I read a two-page dialog passionately because I feel it is one of the best. So does John. When I'm finished Andrew looks tentative. "Nah, too long and boring," he says, "it needs more punch".

I don't agree. I think it's a great dialog because it takes the reader to an inevitable conclusion. Andrew says he doesn't want that, he wants to publish only the inevitable conclusion. "The book has to be a collection of diamonds," he explains, "one explosive pearl of wisdom after the other."

I don't agree. "That's indigestible for the reader" I say, "like baking a chocolate cake with chocolate as its only ingredient." I passionately argue my case. Both John and Andrew seem taken with my reasoning. Or is there something else in their eyes? Am I doing something wrong? In any case, the dialog is decimated as Andrew wants.

John, Robert and I continue our office sessions on the book. But something is slowly changing. I begin to feel increasingly locked out. John and Robert more and more often agree with each other, with me as a third wheel. I often have the feeling that they represent Andrew's point of view and I don't. I want them to know that I'm to be reckoned with, but the feeling that there is something wrong starts to harden in my belly. Maybe I'm not giving enough. Maybe I should put in more effort. I desperately want to do it right, show Andrew that I am living the teachings.

Meanwhile, the whole administration surrounding the book has become a mess. I'm not very punctual and neat by nature, and I become sloppy. It's almost impossible to keep up with the influx of new transcripts. On top of that I have to work at least twenty hours a week to support myself, whereas John and Robert don't. Should I indicate I have too much on my plate? Should I admit I can't handle the workload?

I start to make mistakes, and people start to notice. I begin to rebel against John and Robert's hegemony, which people are also starting to notice. Sometimes in a meeting we come to a decision about a dialog (John and Robert's vote against mine) and then I neglect to implement the decision. John jokes about it. "Hey Andre," he says with a smile, "are you writing Andrew's book or your own book?"

"Mine of course, which will be much better" I joke back. But soon I won't be joking ...

One evening, when the three of us are working, John puts his pen down.

"Andre, there is something that Robert and I want to talk to you about."

Alert. Red alert. The knot in my stomach tightens.

"Yes?"

"It's come to our attention more and more, that you often don't implement the decisions that the three of us have made. Why is that?"

John looks at me intently though not in an unfriendly manner. Fear creeps in. They're going to find out that I'm not on top of this whole project as I should be.

"Yes, that happened a few times, you're right. I'm sorry. It just slipped through."

"So just sloppiness?"

"Yes."

"Because we also noticed that it was often about decisions that Robert and I liked, and you didn't."

He's right, and I tell him so. I admit to some of my paranoid thoughts about being left out, that I was probably overcompensating.

"Well, that's not very good, Andre," Robert says with a stern face. "This is something that you have to take a stand with. If you don't agree with us you just have to tell us. We work as a team here."

I nod. I'm relieved we're talking about this, even though I don't like being criticized. I promise to take a stand with this. John and Robert tell me to face into it, and I promise to do that as well. On the way home I reflect on my tendency to take too much on my shoulders, my ambition, my sloppiness, and I firmly resolve to change myself.

'Facing into it' has become another common expression within the Sangha. In our men's meetings over the past six months it has become clear that changing is not as easy as Andrew had perhaps led us to believe. In theory we should be able to simply recognize the truth of what is pointed out to us about fear, pride, or aggression, and choose against these things on the spot, never to be troubled by them again. Unfortunately this is never the case. We resist when things are pointed out to us and stick to our old ways. Even when we change on a behavioral level, our deep-seated egocentric motivations stay intact. This is why Andrew puts more and more emphasis on self-inquiry and coming to terms with our most basic motivations. He calls it 'facing everything and avoiding nothing': going to the root of egocentric motivations and pushing ourselves right up to their horribly selfish nature, again and again, until we've become completely disgusted with them. Only such disgust, Andrew says, will motivate us to renounce such impulses the next time they raise their ugly head.

The next morning I am in for an unpleasant surprise. John calls me up. He has spoken about our incident last night with Andrew, and Andrew is enraged. He says I'm on a big ego trip. The matter has suddenly escalated. I break out into a cold sweat. I stammer to John that I will look into this very deeply, that I am very sorry, and so on. I am under the gun. My number has come up, as Andrew used to say. What he means is that a certain egoistic tendency can exist for a while without being noticed, and then suddenly it is exposed. You have to be willing to bear a lot of pressure, even humiliation, if that's what it takes to face into this tendency. Now my arrogance and ambition have been exposed, and I have to sink my teeth into it, not run away from it, stay with the discomfort of all this.

Because Andrew has used the word 'ego trip', I'm a marked man. I have to defend myself in one conversation after another against accusations that I'm editing Andrew's book on my own, that I'm not a team player, that I consider myself better, smarter and superior to John and Robert. I admit that I have been sloppy, that it has all been too much for me, that I've been too proud to admit I was in over my head. But to everyone those things sound like meager excuses. They feel I'm avoiding the real issue: my own megalomania in thinking I know better than Andrew. Sometimes I feel as if I'm stuck in a Kafka novel. I try to speak honestly about what I feel has happened, and it is not enough. I try to tell people what they want to hear, and it is also not enough. There seems to be no way out.

I'm out of touch with the conflict that is beginning to rage inside me. I feel unjustly accused, that what I've done wasn't all that bad. I am angry, and this anger has been building for a while: All the long hours at night working on the book, ignoring my other responsibilities; all the time pushing the edge, going beyond my limits. Something inside me that I have denied for too long wants to break out. Driven by ambition and eagerness to please, I have tried to play the role of the perfect student while working on the book. Now I am making one mistake after the other, even while desperately trying to regain my balance. Of course it hurts to lose my status as a prominent student, to lose Andrew's love and appreciation. I am tired and confused. Every day I have to struggle to survive, and to fix the mistakes I have made on the book.

Later on that week there is another incident. I have mislaid a dialog without telling John that it is missing. Andrew is so furious he won't even speak to me. There's only one thing to do: bring up my situation in the men's meeting in order to come clean with my unconscious motivations and to fully face the insidious reality of my ego trip. I'm worried about how I will do because I'm not actually convinced that my behavior was that terrible. What exactly have I done? Granted, my important role with the book went to my head. Granted, I was so proud of being admitted into the inner circle and started feeling better than others. Granted, pride cometh before the fall. But I can't accept that I was deliberately disfiguring Andrew's book with my own editing, that I was writing my own book. Unless I'm crazy and absolutely out of touch with my own lust for power. These answers won't be popular in the men's meeting. I have an ominous feeling.

* * *

The men's meeting has just been opened. Thirty men sit in a circle on meditation cushions. I raise my hand right away as a sign that I want to speak in the meeting. After several other issues are dealt with, it's time. With sweating hands, quavering voice and bowed head I talk about how much I've been on an ego trip with Andrew's book, how sorry I am, and how terrible I feel about doing something so low. I give the whole story, talk about how I've been trying to look into it but that people feel it hasn't been enough. I ask for their help in getting to the bottom of this.

After about ten minutes I'm done talking. I look up. Thirty faces look at me expressionless. Silence. A knot of fear hardens in my stomach. I feel completely at their mercy. Tonight my fate will be decided. Please let someone say something. Then Robert starts to speak.

"That's all well and good Andre, but I feel what's missing is that you're not really sorry about what you've done. I doubt whether you actually realize what you've done."

My heart is beating wildly. I have to respond.

"Yes I do realize that, Robert. It's terrible what I've done."

But it doesn't sound convincing, not even to me.

"I think you're fooling us Andre. You're playing a very dirty game with us. You're still on an ego trip. You're so arrogant that you still think you can pull the wool over our eyes. Your ego is still fully in control. That's exactly the part of you that has to die, the part that you have to kill."

I find it very painful to hear him speak like this. I feel squashed like a bug. He feels I'm playing a game with them but my own experience is that of utter helplessness. I don't know what to do. I feel I'm coming up short in all possible ways.

I stammer something to Robert about the helplessness that I feel.

"Andre, to you it may feel like helplessness, but to us it comes across as a very aggressive attempt to manipulate. You want us to feel sorry for you, but this is something that you yourself are doing. You are not a victim."

"No, I didn't mean to say that..."

"We all say exactly what we mean to say, Andre. You're just trying to survive intact. Even now you are so arrogant that you think you can talk your way out of this. You're still trying to be clever. Just give it up man! We're not buying that from you anymore."

Silence. I look at the floor; feel the tears welling up. I'm desperate. I have no words for it. As I start to cry, I close my eyes and see only blackness. I wish the ground would swallow me up. I can hardly think clearly. What do they want from me now, a full confession? But a confession of what, that I'm an egomaniac? That I'm not convinced of the fact I'm an egomaniac? That I'm trying to convince myself I'm an egomaniac? I have to say something. I can't let this silence last any longer.

"I don't know what else I can say. I've already said I'm sorry."

"That's not good enough Andre. You're letting us down. We're trying to help you but you don't budge. You're only interested in protecting yourself and keeping your own positive self image intact."

In the end the men give up. The meeting parts in deep silence. No one looks at me on the way out.

* * *

Over the next few weeks more meetings follow. Like a juggler I try to handle my inner conflict, like a survival artist I try to keep the others at bay with excuses. But whatever humility and guilt I present outwardly, no one is convinced. Again and again people stress to me what a mortal sin I have committed and how arrogant I am – while deep inside I don't believe it. And my behavior keeps showing it. I do what I want; I feel that I'm right. My conscious and my unconscious are battling with each other. My left hand doesn't know anymore what the right hand is doing. I resist Andrew intensely – and I resist my own resistance intensely. A war is raging within me, ego against superego, I against Ideal-I. Andrew uses more and more draconian measures. At a Sangha meeting (to which I'm not invited) he calls me a lunatic. He says I'm a very disturbing example of how it's possible to have a brilliant understanding of the enlightenment teachings, and yet be able to act in very selfish and immoral ways. That's why it's absolutely necessary to face everything and avoid nothing, he says.

When words don't help anymore, Andrew wants me to act. He proposes I shave my head. The dreaded moment has finally arrived. It is the last thing I want. But I know refusal is not an option. So I shave my head. Now I too join the head shaving meetings. But the other renunciates look at me with disdain. I'm the lowest of the low in the Sangha hierarchy.

I have to cleanse the book of all the contamination I have caused. John, Robert and I go through each fragment together, hour after hour, day after day, two months in a row. When we're finally finished and the last fragment has been cleansed I write a letter of apology to Andrew, adding that I'm glad that the book has now been cleaned up. This proves to be a faux pas, leading to the following scene:

It's a hot day in June 1990. I'm standing in the phone booth in Corte Madera, in front of the deli. I grab a quarter from my pocket. I just got a message to call John back. While my heart beats wildly I dial the number.

"Hi, this is John."

"Hi John, it's Andre."

"Hi Andre. I think I'll get right to it. That letter that you sent yesterday, that was horrible. Andrew and I talked about it, and we don't know what to do with you anymore. Don't you ever learn?"

"What do you mean exactly?"

"What do I mean? Don't play dumb. You know what I mean. Your letter didn't have a speck of humility in it. It's as if you've done this great job to clean up the book, what a great guy you are. Should we all admire you now? You're a megalomaniac, isn't there anything that can get you to consider that maybe you're not God's greatest gift to mankind?"

"But I did apologize in the letter for what I had put you through..."

"Andre you have no idea what you put us through. The past months you have been nothing but trouble. We had to pull all the information out of you while you were only resisting. That the work is finished now is not thanks to you. It's in spite of you! And the book hasn't been cleaned up at all, we have to start from the beginning again now! We have lost four months because of you!"

I feel a sharp pang of anger. "That's not true, dickhead" I think. "It was you and Andrew who found it so necessary to reexamine every piece of paper that had gone through my hands. Ridiculous. Absurd. You could have continued with the book four months ago. So don't blame me."

But I'm too tired to protest. I've argued with John too many times, tried to explain that I only wanted to help, what's the use of it now? John only gets madder when I argue with him.

"Yes you're right John. I'm sorry."

"You're sorry? What kind of bullshit is that? You're not sorry at all. You don't even realize what you've done."

"No, I don't realize what I've done. I'm very sorry."

"You are a sucker, a loser and a pathetic liar. I don't have a speck of respect left for you."

I don't have a speck of respect left for myself by now. I'm too worn down to even defend myself. Let him butcher me.

"I want you to write an apology, not just to me and Andrew, but to everyone in the community. And to prevent you from lying again and showing yourself off as better than you are, I will dictate what you should write. Get some pen and paper."

I grab my bag next to me. Everything's fine with me. As long as John hangs up that phone quick.

"OK, write down: 'I apologize to you all from the bottom of my heart for the suffering that I have imposed on you. Because of my megalomaniacal ego trips and my insidious pride I have robbed you of the precious gift of Andrew's book. I am completely mad and an utterly corrupt human being that I steeped so low. I beg you all for forgiveness,' - no, cut that - 'Although I know I don't deserve it, I beg you all for forgiveness for all the evil wrongdoings I've imposed on you because of my lust for power and my lies. With my deepest apologies, Andre'."

"I wrote it all down, John. I'll do it."

"I'm not finished Andre. Also I want you to buy every single person in the community a bunch of flowers, with a handwritten copy of this letter with it. Tomorrow morning."

"OK John."

Yes John, no John, sorry John, anything you want John. But please let this phone conversation be finished.

John hangs up the phone, and I stand in a daze in the phone booth. Then I stumble outside. I feel utterly humiliated, as if my deepest essence has been so eaten away as not to exist anymore. But I will do it, I know. It is the only thing that I still can do, at least make a good faith effort, and prove I'm willing to do what it takes. Outer obedience is the only thing I can't fail at.

I write eighty letters by hand and buy eighty bunches of flowers. Tomorrow I will drive to all the community houses and deliver the flowers and the letters, and get rehabilitated in that way. I'm so busy with all this that I have little time to think of anything else, yet a small voice within manages to get through to my consciousness. Why am I doing all this? Is Andrew doing this to help me? Or am I being punished? Disturbing questions that I don't pursue further...

3.2 First Crisis of Faith

I complete my flower mission and now I finally have some rest. No one bothers with me any longer. Excreted from the community, fallen from my pedestal, the other community members don't know what to do with me. They feel that I have inflicted great suffering upon Andrew, without showing remorse. My deepest fear is that Andrew will send me away, as he has so many others. At the same time I'm thinking myself about leaving. A popular song in those days is a number from The Clash. I keep hearing the refrains "Should I stay or should I go? If I go there will be trouble, if I stay it will be double".

July 1990, I'm sitting opposite Harry on a bench at a picnic table in the park in Corte Madera. It is Sunday afternoon. In the distance a soccer game is going on.

"What do you want to do now?" Harry asks.

Yes, that's a good question. I live alone now in a garden shack in Mill Valley, as a kind of hermit, feeling depressed and squashed. Andrew has said that I'm not allowed at the men's meetings anymore, and can't live with other community members. That's fine with me. I prefer to be alone.

"Do you want to go back to Amsterdam?"

I look at him. I know what he means. The story of Sariputra and Mogallana. Am I forsaking our common mission?

"No," I say, "I'm going through a difficult period now, but I want to get through it. What that means practically I don't know, but I want to face myself. I feel furious inside, and I will have to face that."

"What are you furious about?" Harry asks.

I wait a moment before answering him. Shall I tell him the whole story? That I'm furious about the rude way I've been treated? That I find it preposterous to crush someone the way they've done with me? That I wonder how a supposedly enlightened man like Andrew can tolerate or even encourage it? Harry's eyes look at me with their usual sincere expression. He is my friend. But at the same time he's Andrew's student. Suddenly the thought flashes through me that maybe Harry is here on a mission from Andrew, to find out what I'm thinking, about whether I doubt Andrew. I kick myself for my cynicism, but I know it may very well be true.

"That anger that lives in me, that's the voice of my ego that's resisting the pressure that's being put on me to change. My ego doesn't want to change."

"Yes, and?"

I decide to take the leap.

"Yes, and I also am having some doubts."

It's out. I look at Harry a little tense, on my guard, checking out how he will react. The D-word has been mentioned.

Harry nods with understanding.

"Yes, that's normal. We all have that response. You know the mind can come up with the most horrible thoughts and they can be very persuasive. Only the point is where do you stand? Do you believe that those thoughts are the last word? Or do you recognize those thoughts as the ego that is rebelling? You know what Andrew says: 'If you want to be free, indulgence in and preoccupation with doubt can be very dangerous. Be very wary of doubt. Doubt is mechanically produced by the ego, and has nothing to do with discrimination'."

Yes, I know that. It's from one of the thousands of transcripts that I've read. But doesn't Harry want to know what my doubts are about? I start to explain why I have doubts, but he interrupts me.

"I don't have to know what they're about. I'd rather you don't empty the garbage can of your mind. I only want to know whether you recognize it as garbage."

Harry looks at me severely. Suddenly I'm certain. He's here as a representative of Andrew and not as my friend. For him those two roles are probably one and the same. I have to be careful about what I say now.

"Yes I know it's garbage Harry. I just find it hard to keep that perspective. Those thoughts can be so convincing."

Harry nods with understanding.

"I know. We all have that experience. That's why Andrew always says we need two swords, one for our own mind and one for other people's minds."

Encouragingly he looks me straight in the eyes. I realize he is completely sincere. He wants to save me from the garbage in my own mind. There is no way I can talk to him about what's actually going on. If I can't talk to Harry who can I talk to?

So why not just leave? Take the plane back to Amsterdam and be done with it all? Why suffer like crazy, be pushed around like this? I consider my situation. I'm 27 years old. For the past three years I've been living in a modern-day monastery, living for God. The living reality of enlightenment has been experientially revealed to me, not only when I met Andrew, but time and time again afterwards. Even if it strikes me as crazy to continue in a situation where I can't even speak freely to my best friends like Harry, I am still fundamentally convinced that Andrew's message is true. His teaching is in my blood, in my very cells.

Yes, now I feel humiliated, trampled, mistreated – but isn't that just the voice of my whining ego, feeling sorry for itself; the voice of the enemy that must be strangled?

I had been reading transcripts of Andrew's dialogs day in day out for nine months, several hours a day: The importance of wanting to be free more than anything else; the law of volitionality, taking responsibility for all our actions no matter how victimized we may feel; facing everything and avoiding nothing, no matter how painful. This is still my mission. However much I feel personally humiliated, I still trust Andrew.

I determine to do whatever it takes to get through this. I won't bail out like so many others because they couldn't take the pressure. I'll suffer the pains of Andrew's purification process rather than returning to an insignificant and mediocre life only aimed at satisfying my own desires. I'll prove to Andrew that I am still faithful to him and his mission.

3.3. Rebirthing

"Those who have a Why can endure any How"
                                                      - Nietzsche

Andrew has been away on a teaching trip and has returned to Marin. As satsang starts up again, I write Andrew a letter, asking him if I can return to the Sangha, and if not, at least attend satsang. His answer takes my breath away. There's no way I can return to the Sangha now, and I also don't deserve to come to satsang. My stubbornness is unparalleled, and he feels that emotionally I'm completely out of touch with the enormity of my resistance and rebellion. He had considered a few weeks ago to have me do a rebirthing session to bring me back in touch with my feelings, but it's too late for that. Only a very strong medicine could help now. Andrew tells me to do one hundred rebirthing sessions with a rebirthing therapist. On that condition, I'm allowed to attend satsang once a week. When I'm finished with the rebirthing sessions, I can apply again to return to the Sangha. It's dizzying. Rebirthing is an intense form of therapy. The thought of a single session fills me with dread, let alone one hundred. On the other hand I feel relieved that Andrew offers me a chance to get out of the current impasse. I make an arrangement with a therapist to do one hundred sessions for five thousand dollars. A voice inside wonders whether this is therapy or punishment; to help me or to have me repent my sins. But predominant is the relief that I'm still allowed to somehow be part of it all. That other voice is the voice of my ego; it's the voice that I have to take a stand with.

Rebirthing is a form of psychotherapy for some and a religious path for others. It's a technique in which you hyperventilate intentionally for three-quarters of an hour. Because of the excess oxygen very strong emotions are released. It has often been claimed that many people re-experience their own birth, the journey through the birth canal. I don't have such experiences in my sessions, but they are intense. The first five are very emotional. All my pent up anger comes out. It is liberating to be able to yell and scream all I want. After that the sessions are less emotional, but I encounter deeper levels of resistance within myself. The pattern of all the sessions is very similar. After about ten minutes of intensive breathing I become extremely sleepy, as if I literally want to avoid the present moment. My therapist encourages me to just continue with the intensive breathing. Whatever my experience is, it's not analyzed. It is just a matter of breathing through it. After thirty to forty minutes the sleepiness gives way to a euphoric feeling. Regardless of whether its cause is an excess of oxygen in the blood, or breathing through negative emotions, it's a fantastic experience. Rebirthing-adepts call this a biological experience of God. Whatever it is, it is a welcome change after the misery of the past months. During the hundred sessions I start to build the confidence that whatever turbulent emotions or thoughts I may experience, I can breathe through it and come out on the other side. I'm no longer afraid of the intensity of my emotions.

During the nine months that the hundred rebirthings take, I live alone in the garden house with a quiet and settled life rhythm. There is no hectic community life with its meetings, endless volunteer work, and continuous social interaction. In the evenings I often sit out in the garden and look at the stars. Images of my life pass before me: The seeker full of longing who sees himself as a freethinker, yet still gives away his heart and soul to a shepherd in order to reach God, and who has now been radically put in his place by that shepherd. To reach God, this seeker himself has to die. He has to cut into his own flesh. The striving to excel, to shine, is in the way. Not my will, but Thy will be done. Noble, idealistic thoughts, but the human drama that has taken place leaves me with questions about Andrew. Why did he never once talk to me in person during this crisis? Why couldn't I explain to him what I was thinking and feeling? My heart yearns to talk with him, to let him take away my doubt. As a guru he doesn't want to relate to his students on the level of their ego. Their projections are their own problems. But these explanations don't take away my feelings. I miss his friendship. But he doesn't seem to need any friends. His love and friendship for his students is conditional. Whoever shows himself to be a loyal student is his friend. Those who are disloyal or unreliable fall out of favor. I wonder – a shocking, disrespectful thought – whether Andrew as a human being is even capable of friendship. That would presuppose equality, and mutual vulnerability.

I think about how everyone wants me to feel remorse for what I've done to Andrew. But I still don't feel I've sinned. Why does Andrew have such a strong reaction to my transgression? Is it such a horrible one? When an ambitious young man, eager to please, is put on a top project, isn't it predictable that some ego-inflation occurs? If I had stayed with NCR to become a project manager, wouldn't a similar thing have happened? Isn't this the normal process of growing up, the fine-tuning of youthful overconfidence? I feel sad and hurt, let down by Andrew. I gave him my heart and my soul, and he's not treating them with much care. I think: Andrew gave me so much responsibility, without support, without a safety net, to let me work sixteen hours a day, driven by ambition and the will to succeed. Isn't it his job to recognize this ambition and drive to succeed, and help me with it? I don't feel helped, I only feel cut down harshly. My thoughts go back to all those others that I cut down harshly when I was still on the other side of the divide. Do I have a right to pity myself? Was Luna right after all? Has Andrew's revolution deteriorated into a fascist community? But of course I can't share such thoughts with the others. They would call me a traitor. Others have been sent away by Andrew for less. It is difficult to even allow these thoughts within myself. These are direct doubts regarding Andrew and his revolution. They only arise because I want to justify myself, because I don't want to admit that Andrew is right. And so I try to convince myself.

Those happy evenings in the Staatsliedenbuurt in April 1987 seem so far away now. In meeting Andrew, there had been such a profound experience of realizing my true nature, of my seeking coming to rest. All of life suddenly seemed so easy, so simple. It would be a matter of sharing the wonderful secret of enlightenment with like-minded souls from all around the world. But now it all has become so much more complicated. So many things I'm not sure about anymore. I feel bad that I'd been so cold and uncaring towards Gina. I should have stood up for our love, regardless of what others would have thought. Was this my ego showing its ugly nature? Hadn't I been too eager in accepting the role of a loyal soldier in the revolution for the sake of enlightenment? Sometimes I feel like an 'organization man' or a politician, who sacrifices his personal values to those of the group.

Yet, all these things that I'm not proud of, are all the more reason to wholeheartedly give myself to purification. If I've been so inhuman at times, I need Andrew's teachings more than ever.

Amidst all these doubts and uncertainties, I still feel love for Andrew. I still feel that he is my teacher; I still feel one with him and that he wants the best for me. I go to satsang once a week and am moved every time by the truth and force of his words, but especially by the power of his silence and the love that speaks to me through that silence. It's not love for me as a person, but love for my deepest essence that radiates from Andrew.

Yes, impersonal love. That's what it must be.

In March 1991 the hundred rebirthing sessions are over. I decide to take a stand with my doubts about Andrew and the treatment I've received. My love for Andrew, my trust in him, and my spiritual longing are stronger than any objections my rational mind can conjure. I surrender myself to that longing, and decide to go for it in spite of what my mind says. The effect is powerful. I feel catapulted into a high energetic state of flow. I have broken through the shackles of my doubt. I'm back in the perspective; ready again to break through my limitations. The past is not an obstacle; the future is not to be feared. There is only the limitless potentiality of the moment right here and now. I have found myself again.

Now I know what it means to conquer myself, to fight my way back to Andrew's perspective no matter what. It is this 'no matter what' that makes Andrew's teaching truly absolute and unconditional. I write Andrew a letter:

"I realize that up to nine months ago my primary focus was to be capable, intelligent and superior to other people, and I even put my intellectual understanding of the Dharma in service of that. When it really came down to me, my character, my integrity, I discovered that I was a failure as a human being. And in the past nine months that has stayed with me continuously. The rebirthing sessions showed me very painfully what an enormous price I had paid for siding with my mind. Suddenly all those tales about the devil, and selling one's soul to him, began to make sense to me, because I found him right inside me. Completely unscrupulous, ruthlessly manipulative, deeply mistrustful, frightfully persuasive and convincing, deeply suspicious and hostile towards everything that is beautiful – that is the enemy that I had given control of my life to. It was shocking to see how much corruption had pervaded my whole life. To conquer this enemy is worth everything to me – I am not afraid to suffer anymore.

"My gratitude for your presence, your care, your help, your love, has been growing like an avalanche. Nobody in this world knows what the mind really is, and what it can do. You gave me the opportunity to discover that for myself, even after I ignored you and so many others who had been shouting this truth at me. I can never thank you enough."

The letters ends with a declaration of love:

"I love you more than I can say Master. You are my very lifeblood. You are the sun that lights up my world. You are the center of my universe. I love you."

With this letter I firmly align myself with the perspective of the community. Through the grapevine, I hear that Andrew is absolutely thrilled with my letter— he's even called it 'cosmic'.

4

ENLIGHTENMENT WARS

Every aspect of our personal experience is ultimately completely impersonal. There is only one human experience, but everybody believes their experience to be unique to them alone.

-Andrew Cohen

4.1. From Personal to Impersonal Enlightenment

It is March, 1991. Andrew has just returned from teaching in Bodh Gaya, a small village in Bihar, the poorest area of India. Bodh Gaya is traditionally known as the place where the Buddha reached enlightenment. It is a place of pilgrimage for Buddhists of many stripes. Perhaps here the *crème de la crème* of spiritual seekers will be found that are receptive to Andrew's message. The whole Californian community has gone with him, except for me and a few others who have been sent out of the community. Of course I'm dying to hear how it went.

Harry and I sit opposite each other in La Petite, an intimate restaurant in Mill Valley. It is my favorite restaurant, near the apartment I share with two other friends who also want to apply for readmission into the community. Harry has a Black Russian sandwich and I have a Club California, with extra avocado.

Harry is full of stories about Bodh Gaya. The whole Sangha had been there—well, mostly.

"It was incredible there Andre, every night satsang!"

"Were there many people from outside the Sangha there?"

"No, not really, it was mainly us."

"And the teachings, Harry?"

Harry swallows a bit of his sandwich and says:

"Well, in Bodh Gaya Andrew complained that after four years of giving satsang, we weren't getting it at all. He's been thinking more about the difference between him and us, why it was that he never fell from grace and we kept stumbling all the time. Why is it that for some people a single glimpse of Reality produces enlightenment but for most people this is not the case? And the Buddha addressed that very same question. He had said that it has to do with karma, with the evolutionary status of a particular person. A highly evolved person would only need to hear the teaching of enlightenment once, and it would affect him profoundly and lastingly. Something like this had happened to Andrew. At the other end of the spectrum were people who were very caught up in the world and in a materialistic lifestyle who would not be receptive to the message at all. And in between there would be all varying gradations of evolution. These people would be receptive to the message of enlightenment, but to varying degrees."

"Yes, but the Buddhist have a different idea of what enlightenment is than the Advaita Vedantists. They say that it's not just about recognizing our own true nature. It's about reaching a state of purity. That's the end result of the spiritual path, when all karmic obstacles have been burned up. Enlightenment is for them some kind of permanent final state from which no falling back is possible, a state of purity where you don't have a shadow anymore."

"Yes, that's it, exactly. That's why Andrew doesn't fall back and we do. He has reached that final purity and we still have lots of impurity inside ourselves. That's why he's permanently enlightened and we've got only glimpses of it, which we're struggling to live up to."

I'm silent for a while, lost in my own thoughts. I think about how Andrew used to stress the fragility of his enlightened state. "I can fall at any moment," he used to say. Often he would express amazement and wonder that he hadn't fallen, that for some miraculous reason he kept walking a straight line, making the right choices, doing the right things, leaving behind him not a trail of confusion and misery like so many other gurus, but a trail of sanity.

Harry breaks the silence.

"One of the Tibetan lamas that Andrew met with, Chatrul Rinpoche, said the same thing, that not everyone's the same. Most people need spiritual practice to overcome their karmic obstacles. Andrew said that he understood for the first time why the Buddha formed a spiritual community and initiated monks, and why he encouraged people to leave the world behind."

"But what does Poonjaji think of all this? This is very different from what he teaches. He's more on the side of Ramana Maharshi."

"Yes, well, that Poonja, there's something fishy going on with him." Harry says it with sudden contempt in his eyes. He doesn't use the affectionate 'ji' anymore that has been customary in the Sangha. I've heard rumors over the past months that things weren't going so well anymore between Andrew and Poonjaji, but because I've been out of the Sangha I didn't know exactly how.

"Poonja behaved very strangely towards Andrew and us. Andrew wanted to introduce his whole Sangha to Poonja, but when we were all in Lucknow, Poonja made up all kinds of excuses to not meet us. He said he was ill, or that he had guests. On the third day we finally just went. We took taxis to Poonja's house and went to his doorstep."

"And what did Poonjaji say?"

"He wasn't there. He was taking a walk. So we just sat down and waited for him."

"And then?"

"Poonja did receive us in the end and was very polite. But we still had a bitter taste in our mouth. I think he's jealous of Andrew's Sangha."

"But Poonjaji has always said that he didn't want a Sangha?"

"Yes, but I think secretly he does."

"So what does Andrew think about all this?"

"He confronted Poonja, but Poonja told Andrew that he didn't need to worry about anything. Then we heard that Poonja said in one of his satsangs that he was looking for lions and not for sheep. We all felt that he was criticizing Andrew behind his back."

* * *

It is not only the personal relationship between Andrew and Poonja which is deteriorating. Andrew also distances himself more and more from Poonja's teachings. In satsang someone asks Andrew how he thinks about Advaita Vedanta. He's very blunt.

"I don't think the Advaita teachings take you all the way. They can give you a glimpse of enlightenment, but they don't transform you."

"Why is that?"

"Well, Advaita teaches what I call 'personal enlightenment'. It's basically about *my* enlightenment, *my* realization, the end of *my* suffering. As long as you're fundamentally still out for yourself, how can you ever be radically transformed? The ego will still be running the show; it will take hold of anything, even enlightenment."

"So what would it mean then to be radically transformed?"

"This is what I call 'impersonal enlightenment'. You're not out for your own benefit, but you feel compelled by an evolutionary urge deep within yourself to transcend your petty little personal perspective, and realize a far bigger possibility, for the sake of the human race. But such a realization is not just some experience of bliss. It only has any meaning if it radically transforms you, if it wipes out any trace of a personal agenda."

"That sounds very different."

"It's completely different. It's the difference between a burning match and a forest fire."

"Does it have anything to do with what the Buddhists call no-self, the idea that there is no such thing as a stable self?"

"Yes, very much. We only think of ourselves as a unique individual person because we've been taught that that's what we are. But actually this habit of looking at our experience and ourselves from a personal perspective is one of the major obstacles in spiritual life. Because we identify with thoughts and feelings as 'my thoughts' and 'my feelings' we contract and form a protective shell around ourselves. Then we put a lot of energy into maintaining and defending this imaginary sense of self. But if we really pay close attention, there is nothing in our experience that is personal in any way. Everything that we think and feel is an impersonal response to impersonal circumstances. There is no such thing as an 'I' that thinks our thoughts and feels our feelings. They just come and go."

In the silence that hangs in the air after these words, I let them sink in. This personal and impersonal enlightenment business reminds me of the two major Buddhist schools, Theravada (the Indian vipassana tradition that Andrew was originally involved in) and Mahayana (as emphasized in Tibetan Buddhism). Personal enlightenment corresponds to the Theravada ideal of the arhat, who is striving for nirvana (enlightenment) for himself, whereas impersonal enlightenment corresponds to the Mahayana ideal of the bodhisattva, who, out of universal love and compassion for all sentient beings takes a vow not to enter nirvana until all other beings have reached it. Andrew sounds like he's turning into a Mahayana Buddhist. I'm fascinated but also a bit apprehensive. Is he putting himself above his own guru and the entire tradition of Advaita Vedanta?

4.2. Parting of the Father and the Son

The widening gap between Andrew's new teaching and Advaita Vedanta doesn't go unnoticed by the spiritual seekers who come to satsang. Many of them come expecting to find a teacher of enlightenment who will give them a profound spiritual experience. Instead they're told off about their lack of willingness to change themselves. Many people perceive this as a kind of moralizing they can do without, and decide to go to the source itself, and visit Poonja in India, as do some of the students who've been sent away from the community by Andrew. To their relief, and to Andrew's displeasure, they receive a warm welcome there. Some of them, having received Poonjaji's enlightenment, are sent back to the West to teach others. The most important of these is an American woman named Antoinette Varner, who had been with Andrew in satsang for a few months before going off to see Poonja. Poonjaji gives her the name Gangaji and sends her out to teach in the places that Andrew has just been teaching. He tells her to "clean up after Andrew," restore the proper understanding of Advaita Vedanta, and heal any egos that have been wounded. We hear that Poonja speaks about us as "sheep" that merely follow an authority, which he considers antithetical to true freedom and enlightenment.

Gradually Poonja starts to attract more and more followers while the number of Andrew's students seems to remain the same. The loving father-son relationship appears to be turning competitive. Andrew feels betrayed by his teacher, feels there's a war going on with the Advaita Vedanta establishment.

Also in the Sangha there's a war going on: the war against the ego. Because of Andrew's new emphasis on impersonal enlightenment, the process of purification takes on a new and heightened significance. It is not only for our personal benefit, but for the evolutionary development of the whole human race. Andrew starts to look for methods that are powerful enough to facilitate the kind of transformation that he has in mind. Though there's still the old antagonism with some of the western Buddhist meditation scene, Andrew becomes interested in Tibetan Buddhism. In April 1990, in Boulder, Andrew meets with former students of Trungpa in satsang, and several join the Sangha. Then, in January 1991, in Bodh Gaya, Andrew meets with several well-known lamas. He has one of his booklets translated into Tibetan. The dialogs with the Tibetan Buddhists pique his interest in the Tibetan system with its many practices such as mantras, prostrations, meditation, scriptural study, much of which Andrew eventually adapts to his own teachings. During the Bodh Gaya retreat he begins to practice formal meditation with his students, one hour every morning. Back in Marin this pattern continues. Gradually the emphasis on purification and the burning up of karmic tendencies intensifies through spiritual practices.

From 1991 on, community life becomes established in spiritual practice, usually about two or three hours a day. These spiritual practices work. They strengthen the familiar sense of conquering yourself, of being stronger than your resistance. You have no time for doubt, and completing your practice gives you a sense of accomplishment and achievement. This helps to stay in the perspective, the exhilarating feeling that no obstacles exist, anything is possible and nothing is outside your grasp. It is a great rush of power. After you've done your five hundred prostrations in the morning with your housemates, you have coffee together at 7 a.m., feeling great and ready to conquer the world.

Andrew then introduces yet another new practice: giving names to students who prove very resistant. A man with a temper is called Raging Bull; an immature student is called Q the Clown, a woman who tends to space out is called Dizzy. Later on this is followed by names like Unreal, Sincere, His Greatness, etc. The names are meant to bring about humility by continuously reminding the student of the vicious patterns that he's unwilling to let go of.

Andrew attaches a lot of importance to the intellectual understanding of his teachings, and the ability to express them clearly and objectively. One method to achieve this is the discussion group. In 1992, students begin to meet in groups of six to ten, to discuss an excerpt of his book *Enlightenment is a Secret*. Often the excerpt is discussed sentence by sentence. Later, in 1993 and 1994, these groups are ordered hierarchically and led by senior students. At the end of the meeting everyone is evaluated: how much did we participate, how clear, original, and powerful was our expression of our understanding of the excerpt. The ones who do well are put in a higher group the next week; the ones who don't go to a lower group. The whole program is administered by a group of senior students. I'm usually pretty good in these groups, and manage to stay in the higher groups.

4.2. What is Enlightenment?

By November 1991, the 'war' against Poonja and Advaita Vedanta fills the air. Since the spring I've been making my way back into the community. I'm living in a community house again but at a lower level than before. I'm going to all the meetings. The phone in our house rings and it's Andrew. He wants to speak to me. Nervously, I take the phone. I've hardly had any personal contact with him since the whole drama surrounding his book.

"Listen, Andre," he says, "you know how Poonja and the whole Advaita Vedanta scene have been jerking me around. Nobody really understands what I'm teaching. I want to do something about it. We're going to set up a journal with articles about my teaching, interviews with other teachers, and so on. It will be called *What Is Enlightenment?* and it will be dedicated to the question of what enlightenment actually is."

"That sounds great Andrew," I say. "It's a great way to bring your teachings out in the open, and to correct the misunderstanding and the false allegations about you."

"Yes, don't you think? It's going to come out once every six months. And listen, I want you to work on it. I want you to be the editor-in-chief."

I can't believe my ears. I'm getting a new assignment, a chance to rehabilitate myself.

"Thank you, Andrew," I say, "that's very generous of you."

I couldn't be happier. This is my chance to prove that I can work in a team, that I can be trusted to deliver good work, that I'm a changed man. I assure Andrew that he can count on me.

"Really?" he says, "I am still not convinced, but John and Robert wanted me to give you another shot. I feel like I'm giving a bottle of whisky to an alcoholic."

He laughs and hangs up the phone. I rush to the flower store to buy him a bunch of flowers. One and a half years after my fiasco he's giving me another chance!

Before long I am at work again in the familiar community office, with John, Robert, and all the people that I knew so well from working on the book. One of the main subjects of this first issue is the disagreement between Andrew and Advaita Vedanta about personal versus impersonal enlightenment. Just as Andrew had challenged the Buddhists for their complacency in the beginning, he is now taking on the Advaita Vedantists. He questions the Advaita teachings because they leave a lot of room for corruption. Because the personality is not real,

Advaita-adepts can get away with anything, with immoral behavior, selfishness that causes suffering for others. Advaita-adepts would say that we can not judge human actions. They would ask, "Who's judging?" Andrew mocks this endlessly in his public teachings and in the Sangha meetings. He calls it "The advaita shuffle," in which the Advaita teachings of Oneness are misused to justify all kinds of unethical behavior. I write the editorial for the issue, introducing the theme and summing up the various articles. Andrew provides a transcribed tape recording of his public discussion with Gangaji. I also write an article with another student based on this transcript to illustrate how ludicrous Gangaji is and how irrational her "advaita shuffle".

The first draft of my editorial is met positively by Andrew and the others, they feel it's eighty percent finished, but when I submit the second draft, they feel I've not implemented their suggested improvements in a satisfactory way.

Now a familiar scene takes place. At a meeting at Andrew's house he says to me, "Your first draft was very good, but what you've done with it now really sucks." I swallow. I've been working on it for days. "I've decided to not take any more risks," he says, "considering what happened in the past." He has another student finish the editorial. I'm crushed. Once again I've proven myself unreliable, not to be able to fulfill my promise. I feel ashamed and disappointed, but I'm also furious. All the strong feelings from last year resurface. All the questions that I stuffed away in a dark corner are coming out again. Did Andrew just use me again? I dropped everything else in my life, all too eager to please him, to prove myself to him. Does Andrew only appreciate me insofar as my intellectual performances can be of help to him and his projects? Am I his beloved student, or some kind of intellectual prostitute? I have a difficult time dealing with the inner demons that are resurfacing. The other students give me a hard time because I've blown it, because I've let Andrew down. I have to face into my own unreliability, they say. I have to take responsibility.

In spite of my flunked editorial for the first issue, I continue to be on the editorial staff of *What is Enlightenment?* until 1994. The journal, an eight-page newsletter to begin with, would turn into a full-color magazine with an ever-increasing circulation. It remains to this day.

In the wake of his war against Poonja, Andrew broadens his crusade against the corruption he observes in the wider spiritual world as well. In his 1992 book *Autobiography of an Awakening*, Andrew describes his breakup with Poonja, and sets down his manifesto for the crusade. It's a sharp indictment of nearly all the modern day gurus and spiritual teachers in view.

4.4. Doing Battle in the Katmandu Retreat

Soon after my journal crisis, in early January 1992, we go off to Bodh Gaya again for Andrew's now yearly retreat. This time I go as well, my first time in India. The third world surroundings distress me. Beggars continually assault me; I see dead bodies lying on the streets; the entire atmosphere is one of terrifying chaos. It matches the chaos inside me. In the ever-dusty little streets of Bodh Gaya, I walk around like a shadow, unhappy, ill at ease with myself. I'm still shaken by my failure and subsequent dismissal as a journal-editor. In the lower-level community group that I'm part of now we have a men's group of six. Andrew has us have meetings almost every day, and gives us a variety of practices to get us going. He wants us to move up to a higher-level community group, but again and again he feels we are not ready. I'm one of the worst. I'm not going for it. My self-confidence has gone. I feel like a loser. I get sick and spend many days in bed. I lose quite a bit of weight. At the end of Bodh Gaya, I look more like a ghost than a human being.

After Bodh Gaya Andrew goes on to teach in Katmandu for the month of February. He is so unhappy with our men's group that he has us do an intensive silent meditation retreat there for three weeks. We are not to go to the teachings, but live in seclusion and follow an intensive program. Every day we do three hours of meditation, one thousand prostrations, and another three hours of mantra meditation. I get up at four-thirty. I go into a little room with the others where we sit in a circle and chant one of Andrew's texts on clarity of intention out loud. Then I go back to my own room and meditate from five to six. From six to seven-thirty, I do 500 Tibetan-style prostrations on a two by one-meter piece of cardboard. I put a picture of Andrew at the end of my board, so that each time that I lie fully stretched out on the board, I look right at Andrew's broadly smiling face and into his radiant eyes. After a quick shower (500 prostrations is a real workout), we all have breakfast together in silence. At nine-thirty, it is time for mantra meditation. In my room I sit down on a meditation cushion and repeat one of Andrew's texts 54 times. We have three different texts. One of them is the excerpt *"Pride is vicious."* This is the one that gets me going. It is meant to annihilate any sense of individuality, or independent self-existence, since these are the most prominent obstacles to enlightenment. I meditate on these lines:

"Pride is vicious. Pride is the most vicious enemy for those who claim they want to be enlightened in this birth..."

This is true warrior language. I repeat these lines with the intensity of a crusader in a battle field, waving the sword of will power against this vicious enemy. The excerpt goes on:

"Equate pride with whatever you imagine ego to be. Pride and ego are the same thing. . ."

If pride is the same as the ego, it must be killed at all cost. My deepest longing for Liberation, that is the fuel that keeps me going. My own doubts, my mixed feelings during the time of rebirthing that almost caused me to quit, that is the enemy called pride.

"Pride has a very ugly face. Pride is based on the idea that you know something. When you think you know something you feel special, and when you feel special you feel separate. . ."

Well, yes, while working on Andrew's book I definitely thought that I knew something. I even thought I knew better than Andrew at some points. So this is the ugly face that Andrew sees in me. I think I'm better than others, and therefore I make myself separate, betraying the

Oneness that we have all experienced and which is the basis of our being together.

"Ideas of specialness or superiority will separate you from what you claim to want the most. . ."

So this idea that I know something will also keep me from true freedom. And I'm basically contributing to the horrible mess of violence and aggression that I see in the world. All that because I insist that I know better, rather than just giving in and being humble.

"Even for those who are enlightened pride is a difficult obstacle to perfection. . ."

This is why Andrew split up from Poonja. Even a powerfully enlightened man such as Poonja is not free from this.

We have lunch together in silence from twelve to two. From two to three, I meditate again for an hour in my room. Then it is time for 500 more prostrations. From five until five-thirty, we have a tea break. In silence we slowly sip our cups of tea, then, another hour of meditation. This is followed by dinner together in silence and then another hour of meditation. Finally, at ten, we finish the day in our little common room by chanting another of Andrew's inspiring and invigorating excerpts.

In this small room in Katmandu, I find plenty of time to also contemplate more personally. What am I actually doing? I am hurt by my rise and fall in the Journal. It's a kind of miniature repetition of what happened with the book, and it reopens old wounds. All the previous hurt, humiliation and anger flare up again. A thousand times a day, I throw myself down on my prostration board. Each time I go down I see Andrew's face, that boyish grin, that innocent look in his eyes. Who is this man? Is he a saint or a monster? Why do I love him? Why do I want his love and approval so badly, more than anything in the world? Does Andrew actually care about me? Is it all worth it? Shouldn't I be doing something else with my life? These are unspeakable thoughts that I can't discuss publicly. But safe behind the walls of my little room, with no one bothering me or putting pressure on me, I fantasize about returning to Amsterdam, leading my own life, being a writer and philosopher. I could still support Andrew's cause by writing articles and books about him. I could regain mastery of my own life and still keep Andrew's respect and approval. I could have my cake and eat it too.

On the second to last day, my protest reaches its height. I no longer want to be a pawn in Andrew's chess game, a front soldier in his holy war. I decide I no longer want to be Andrew's student, and imagine a life where I myself choose how I live, what I think, and what I believe and don't believe in. I intend to speak to Andrew that same day about this and announce my departure. But our scheduled talk that day with Andrew is cancelled.

The next day, as I prostrate again and again I realize that when it comes down to it, I am still convinced it's the Absolute shining through his eyes. Something beyond the mind is emanating from him. After all is said and done, that's still my bottom line. I'm with Andrew in his revolutionary undertaking. I'm glad I was unable to realize my ill-conceived intention the day before. I write Andrew a love letter, about how he is my shepherd that leads me to safe pastures. I've managed just in time to silence the critical voice of doubt inside me, and now I try to shout over it as loudly as I can.

5

GINA

Romantic life is just two egos worshiping each other.
-Andrew Cohen

From the beginning, Andrew's teachings have had a renunciatory attitude towards sexuality and sexual relationships. Andrew himself is married, several of his students are married, but up to now students have rarely formed new relationships, while other couples have split up because they want to put enlightenment first and feel their attachment to each other is an obstacle. It seemed natural, if painful at times, that the revolution had taken us in this direction, but in January 1993, in a subsequent Bodh Gaya retreat, Andrew changes his approach.

5.1. Sexuality and Impersonal Love

One day I'm sitting with a few other people in the lounge of the Tourist Bungalow, where we are all staying with Andrew, when we see the women students descend the stairs one by one, mute and with heads bowed. The second floor is where Andrew's quarters are. This can mean only one thing: the women have had a meeting with Andrew. And if we can judge by their faces, it hasn't been a pleasant one. Bit by bit I gather what has happened. Andrew has called the women together to challenge them about how they are relating to sexuality. He feels they are avoiding sexuality, and treat it as non-spiritual. That has to change. Andrew wants there to be more sexual relationships in the Sangha. In a subsequent Sangha meeting Andrew explains how he sees it:

"Sexuality is an impersonal force that is part of being human. It's not something to avoid. Of course I think it's positive if people want to be celibate to make their relationship to sexuality less compulsive. But that's not a must. To be active in a sexual relationship can also be a very good way to learn more about sexuality."

Miriam raises her hand.

"But if sexuality is an impersonal force, how can we be in a sexual relationship with a particular person? What determines our sexual preference then?"

Andrew shrugs.

"In a way it's arbitrary who you're in a relationship with. You have to be compatible on a personality level but in principle I think that in this Sangha there's such an intimacy between everyone that in fact everyone could be in a sexual relationship with anyone else."

"But then sexuality has nothing to do with the usual image of romantic love."

"That's right. Romantic love is purely an illusion—just two egos worshiping each other. That's something very different than a mature sexual relationship from an impersonal perspective. When you know that sex is not

114

the most important thing in the world, you won't be that focused on your relationship. Sex doesn't have first priority, but maybe fifth or sixth."

"But sexuality does belong in a monogamous relationship?"

"Yes, I don't believe in promiscuity. It's about manifesting Absolute reality, and that is deeply moral. But tell me, what about you? Do you have anyone in mind?"

The direct question takes Miriam by surprise. She blushes.

"Well, not really..."

"That doesn't sound that convincing. Are you sure?"

"Well, maybe, but..."

"But?"

"It's not really someone I know that well."

Andrew looks at her, and I have the feeling he's about to ask her who it is, in front of everybody. Then he seems to conclude that that could lead to complications and he says, "Okay, we can talk about this later together."

Three days later Miriam and Mick announce that they're now in a relationship. They are going to Varanasi for three days on a "honeymoon." That's big news. So it was Mick. Various people confirm that Miriam and Mick indeed hardly know each other. But that doesn't seem to be an obstacle. Three days later Harry and Sophia also announce they're in a relationship. They're going away for three days on "honeymoon" as well. A few days later Robert announces his relationship with Rudra, also a close student of Andrew.

I'm not sure what to think about all this. This "from zero to hundred" method is kind of radical. I try to imagine myself being in a relationship with someone from one day to the next, without courtship, without flirting, but in the old fashioned way, like an arranged marriage.

Of course this is now the talk of the day within the Sangha. Who will get together with whom? Everyone is aware that Andrew is behind the relationships or at the very least no relationships will be formed without his permission. Yet we speculate among each other about our preferences. I know my own. It is Gina.

5.2. In Love

When Gina had left the community in January 1990, I hardly had time to dwell on it, busy as I was with my glorious book project. But when I had fallen into my own downward spiral a few months later and found myself in the garden house in Mill Valley with ample time for reflection, I had to think again about Gina. I'd been so distant and superior with her, so cold and insensitive, an ambitious social climber. Of course she'd been in love with me and she'd been unable to admit that. I could have helped her if I wouldn't have been so concerned with what the others thought of me. I could have been honest about my own feelings, whether they benefited me socially or not. I felt I had let Gina down. I wrote her a letter explaining this to her. She wrote me a grateful and relieved letter back and also wrote that she wanted to come back into the Sangha. She had gone to the Bodh Gaya retreat in January 1991, and reconnected with Andrew so strongly that he invited her to come back to Marin. In the spring of 1991, Gina came back into the

Sangha, at the time when I was still out in the doghouse. During 1991 and 1992, our positions reversed. Gina was a respected community member, and I was struggling in the lower regions of the community. After my battles in Katmandu, I had slowly made my way back up. By now, in January 1993, we both belonged to the higher strata in the Sangha. Would it now be possible...?

I take my time. I speak about it with my roommates. I have coffee with Gina a few times. Neither of us speaks about the past, but of course it hangs like a cloud over our heads. In April, I take the leap. I write a letter to Andrew about my intention to ask Gina to be in a relationship with me. What does he think? Unfortunately Andrew has just gone to Boulder for three weeks, so I have to wait until he's back before I can speak with him. Gina is also in Boulder to help with setup, so at least I don't have to suffer through trying to act normal with her while being utterly nervous inside.

When Andrew comes back from Boulder I speak with him in a little room behind the satsang hall. He tells me that he has no objections. Excited I walk out of the room. Now things are getting real. I drive home and I can't wait any longer. I call Gina. "Would you like to go for coffee tomorrow?" I ask casually. Of course the casual effect is somewhat lessened by the fact that it's one-thirty in the morning ... "Yes, all right," Gina says, apparently not surprised by the proposal. The next day we meet for coffee, and I pop the big question. She is surprised. She didn't expect I'd be so straightforward about it.

"You're not trying to make up for the past, are you?" she says.

I assure her that it's got nothing to do with that. She asks for time to think about it. I agree and wait nervously. Three days she thinks about it, then, as we sit opposite each other in the same coffee shop, she says "yes." My heart jumps. We look at each other. So now we're a couple. Now what? Buy flowers for Andrew. Good idea. We drive to the flower shop in Sausalito. We call our Sangha houses and tell them the good news. We deliver the flowers to Andrew's house. Then we hear from our houses that they've organized a dinner with both houses in San Rafael. Okay. We are both in a daze, everything's going so fast. I realize we haven't even kissed each other. During the dinner, our friends give speeches. It seems almost like a wedding dinner. Both of our houses play the role of our families that proudly see their son and daughter take off into marriage. That impression gets even stronger when we are presented with a gift at the end of the dinner. A night together in a hotel in Larkspur! We look at each other in shock. Actually we had planned to just go home and have a cup of tea. Now we start to realize that this is going to be our wedding night and that there is sex on the program. Discretely we are handed a bag of toiletries, with condoms and other such invaluable items. This has been prepared well! Who has arranged all this?

Everybody waves us goodbye as Gina and I leave by car to the hotel. We hardly dare look at each other. In the parking lot of the hotel Gina turns off the engine. Silence. Neither of us makes any move to step out of the car. What's the next step? Carefully I take Gina's hand. She accepts my hand and looks at me. This brings back old memories. Slowly, very slowly, we caress. We will work it out together — I know that for sure.

Gina and I spend three days on our 'honeymoon', completely in love with each other. These are among the happiest days of my life. Both of us are floating two inches above the ground.

But once back in the community, we get a message from Andrew. He is upset that we haven't written to him about what it's like being together. We are rudely reminded of the fact that our relationship is not a "personal" one with all the normal romantic illusions involved, but can only occur by the grace of Andrew, and in the context of his community.

Gina moves into my Sangha house. We have our own room, but apart from that we are both to understand there's nothing private or special about our relationship. We flourish. Intimacy and trust grows between us like I've never experienced before. Things are going well for me within the community. Andrew asks me to collect transcribed material for his new book. I become head of the editorial department within the community, coordinating all the transcribers and responsible for the texts for flyers and brochures. Being in a top position in the community gives me a great sense of accomplishment. It's also an affirmation for me that Andrew's teachings work. I feel I've slain my demons and am now finally able to live the teachings. I feel happy now that I hung in there during my crisis with the book and didn't leave.

In January 1994, we all go to Bodh Gaya again. It is a fantastic experience for me. After my hellish experiences in 1992, I've actually grown to like Bodh Gaya. I feel connected with Andrew and his teachings. And it's great to be there with Gina by my side. We're both doing well; there are rumors of us being sent to Europe to lead one of the new centers there. Such a contrast with my Katmandu battles two years ago.

Andrew speaks in his talks about sitting down in meditation, letting the mind quiet down, and letting yourself sink into the ground of being. It's very powerful the way he speaks about it. Several times a day we have meditation sessions; a few hundred people sit cross-legged with closed eyes in a big tent. The experience of the ground of being becomes a tangible and shared experience. Andrew speaks about the essence of life being a positive force, a big "yes." At the core of life there is fundamentally no problem. In the meditations we sink deeply into this experience. It gives us strength to face daily life, where there seem to be endless problems.

After Bodh Gaya we go with a small group to the beach in Thailand for a ten-day vacation. It is paradise there. All my doubts are forgotten. I'm in a great relationship, I'm doing the editorial work that I love, and I'm playing an important role in supporting Andrew's spiritual mission. My life makes sense; it has a purpose. What more could I ask for?

5.3. Gina Goes to Amsterdam

In March 1994, back from the yearly Asian trip, a lot of tasks and responsibilities are waiting in Marin. I'm working on the journal *What is Enlightenment?*, and compiling material for a new book. I'm getting quite overwhelmed by all this and lose my track a bit. In the men's meetings I get feedback for being too preoccupied with my feelings of stress and anxiety.

Then Andrew calls a meeting with the entire Sangha. We've been in Marin for five years now and the community has hardly grown. Andrew's talks draw local people that are interested but very few feel compelled to join the Sangha. Therefore, maybe Europe is where the revolution should happen. Robert and Mick were sent to London in 1993 to establish a center. An organization is set up, Friends of Andrew Cohen in Europe, or FACE. Also in Amsterdam a center is established by local lay students. Gina and I had gone there in the summer of 1993 to help coordinate Andrew's teaching trip.

Another point is that people who do apply for Sangha membership are often turned down because they don't meet the high behavioral standards of the Sangha. To remedy this last situation Andrew has introduced the "formal student program." It is intended for people who are attracted to his teachings but don't yet feel ready to join the Sangha. It involves committing oneself to two hours of meditation a day, and living with other formal students. Formal students are not held to the same high behavioral standards of the Sangha. Since the introduction of the program a few months ago, about forty people have become formal students.

Both new developments change the purpose of the Sangha. More leaders are needed, both to manage the formal student program in Marin, and to assist in the expansion in Europe. The Marin Sangha should be a boot camp of sorts to cultivate such leaders. Therefore the standard must go up. Andrew announces that he will split up the Sangha over the next months: those that prove themselves to be independent leaders can be "committed students," the others can join the formal students.

As usual after such meetings, a period of forced activity and increased ruthlessness begins. Everyone tries to shift into higher gear and wants to prove that they're responding to Andrew's challenge. Gina and I are candidates for leadership of the Amsterdam center, and have to show our leadership mettle. Gina succeeds very well in this. She grows into a leading figure in the women's groups. I myself come into the grips of free-floating anxiety, fearful with a sense of impending doom. On my birthday Gina takes me with her to San Francisco for an outing. She is one big energy bulb, inspired by the ideal of impersonal enlightenment, and the impersonal view. I'm walking around in a cloud of fear and self-preoccupation.

The next day Gina gets a message from Andrew. He wants her to move to Amsterdam in three weeks time to lead the center there with Harry. I can't go with her; Andrew says I'm not ready yet to be a leader. Maybe I can go to Amsterdam in a few months time, if I prove myself. I am stupefied. I don't know what to think or feel. Should I be excited about this opportunity that Andrew is giving Gina, this honorable election? Should I be impressed by Andrew's psychological insight and his daring and incisive action? Or should I be furious about the fact that he sends my girl to Amsterdam without even so much as mentioning it to me first? In Andrew's message of impersonal enlightenment it's very obvious that our personal agenda, what we personally think and feel, is always secondary to the bigger picture.

I feel tormented. I'm excited about Andrew's revolution, and I want to participate wholeheartedly in it. I want to live the impersonal teachings, want to purge myself of any selfishness. I know the revolution asks big sacrifices of us all, that we have to renounce our longings for a personal life; that it's about something much bigger than our own petty desires. And yet on the other hand I am angry. Not even so much about the fact that he wants to send Gina to Amsterdam without me, but about the way in which he does it. If Andrew would have sat down with the two of us, would have consulted us, I would have felt better about it. Old doubts are resurfacing. What is Andrew's motivation for this decision? Does he want to teach me a lesson? Or does it have nothing to do with me? Is he merely looking for someone that he can use in Amsterdam? This decision of Andrew's feels wrong, but is it only my attachment to Gina speaking here? Can I trust my own intuition? My doubts fill me with fear. I don't want to open up Pandora's box here. Maybe I'm unwilling to live Andrew's teachings. Maybe I don't want to kill my ego. Maybe I do want a life for myself. But I don't want to weaken my conviction in Andrew and his teachings. I desperately want to believe.

My inward torment paralyzes me. But I can't afford to be paralyzed. I have to respond. Andrew will be curious as to how I'm taking the news, and my response will reveal where I'm at. So I hastily compose a message to Andrew that I call in to the community office. The message says how excited I am that Gina is going to Amsterdam and that I look forward to joining her there soon.

Harry answers the phone in the office, and he listens to my message approvingly. But concerning the last phrase about me joining her soon he says, "Well, don't take anything for granted there."

As a good student I have outwardly expressed my appreciation and enthusiasm for Andrew's plan, but inwardly I'm furious. I feel Andrew is playing with me. I feel as if his implicit message to me is "if you want to keep your girl friend, you better get over your insecurity and anxiety and become a leading figure; then you can go to Amsterdam too."

I manage to keep myself together in the three weeks that I still have left with Gina. The evening before she leaves for Amsterdam there is a party. She gets presents and there are speeches. I'm sitting in the midst of the other community members with a broken heart. But if I show it, I definitely do not have an impersonal relationship to my emotions and wouldn't have a chance of being sent to Amsterdam too. I keep up a good appearance and even manage to bring out a toast for Gina. The smile on my face feels more like a frozen grin. The next day I take her to the airport. We both cry, as if we know in our hearts that this will be farewell. I feel like I'm losing my girlfriend to the revolution. In the way back in the car I feel how angry I am. I feel powerless. Andrew holds all the cards. I can do nothing but play the game on his terms.

During the next months I try my best to show what a leader I can be. But my inner conflict is not resolved. And it shows. More often than not others tell me that they feel my heart is not really in the community. They could be right. Within me a sense of rebellion rages.

In my work on the Journal, as with the work on Andrew's book, a kind of self-sabotage takes place. I manage to forget things, which drives Andrew up the wall. All my efforts seem forced, unreal. As the pressure to change, to give more, to be more wholehearted increases, I grow more stubborn. In my most rebellious moments I think, they can get my time and my efforts, but my heart they'll never get. Gina hopes I will be sent to Amsterdam too, but the harder I try to prove my leadership potential, the clearer it becomes to everyone how unreal that is.

In a Sangha meeting Andrew finally chastises me for my emotional instability. "You're an emotional basket case," he says, "very weak emotionally. How could I send you to Amsterdam? How could you be a leader there? They would all see through you in no time." I nod. I feel humiliated and defeated. Andrew continues.

"You're so intelligent," he says, "and I want to make use of it. But because of your emotional instability I can't. It's so frustrating!"

I nod again and say nothing. He surely must know I'm furious with him? It seems the only thing he's interested in is whether he can use my capacities for his projects. I feel I'm being used.

5.4. John's Demise

In the midst of my struggle, there is other disturbing news. John, Andrew's top student, his right hand man and best friend, is not doing well. Andrew feels he's too immature and arrogant. Andrew says that John is not his own man, not a leader. He says John emulates all the qualities of a leader, but there's not enough real substance behind it. Yet, my inner companion, Doubt, never completely absent since the drama around the book, wonders how you can become your own man when you're the right hand man to a dominant leader like Andrew. Doesn't 'becoming your own man' mean growing into your individuality? Isn't that only possible when you can make your own decisions and mistakes? When all your choices and decisions are prescribed according to 'the impersonal perspective', which basically means according to Andrew's rules, Doubt says, the best you can become is an efficient enforcer, never your own man.

My struggle against Doubt increases when the only man who seemed exempt from the law, under which everybody falls sooner or later, now falls himself. Andrew is putting enormous pressure on John and John is not responding, is not coming through.

"Freud said we're all doing the best we can," Andrew says at satsang one night, "but in my teaching that's not good enough." He looks at John in the corner. "Isn't that true, John?"

After we had come back from Asia, I worked with John on the Journal. I found him different, subdued and docile, a shadow of his former self with no self-confidence. Some people said that John's retreat in Asia had changed him, that he had become more humble. I didn't see that. I saw someone who didn't trust himself anymore.

After that Sangha meeting, the drama around John unfolds. Soon we no longer see him around. He's not working on the Journal anymore. He's not at satsang. He doesn't come to meditations. Only a few people know that he is in retreat, in a house somewhere in Corte Madera. Every day John does hours of meditation, tries to face into things, overcome his resistance and take a stand with his pride. Robert or Andrew visits him daily. They plead with him, yell at him, and try anything to get him to respond. But John is not coming through. He has frozen up, he is stuck in his pride, is what the reports say. News about John becomes increasingly scarce. I hear Andrew sends him for a week to a Greek island, to the beach, apparently not with the hoped-for result. John does not return to Marin. A few weeks later we hear that Andrew has sent him away.

Andrew speaks about it in a Sangha meeting. He says how painful it's been for him. All of us are full of support for Andrew, and we admire his uncompromising stance. He even went so far as sending away his best friend, rather than compromising his teaching! Andrew really means it. It's black or white. There's only success or failure. And there's no such thing as doing the best we can. No mercy, no excuses.

But John's downfall is a defining moment. It means that no one is beyond reproach. John was closer to Andrew than anyone. Andrew also yelled at John more than at anyone, always criticizing him, chastising him, demanding more from him. But John could always take it, would always respond, would take it on, and would take more responsibility. He was an example and an inspiration to us, though I have other, mixed memories of him as well. I'm one of the community members who got to know a different side of him, the ruthless prosecutor, the harsh inquisitor. The phone call in front of the deli in Corte Madera still burns in my mind. The only moral justification for such righteous persecution has always been for me that he himself was willing to suffer the agonies of the fight against his own inner demons. But now John is not coming through. It makes me angry, sad and doubtful. If John can't do it, who can? Can I? What is enlightenment if in the end none of us can maintain it? Andrew told us in the beginning that we were already enlightened. Is that true, or did we have only momentary glimpses? Are we all only on the path to enlightenment, just as the Buddhists say?

5.5. Second Crisis of Faith

Meanwhile, I have plenty of my own problems to think about. Andrew's public rant against me has made me a marked man once again. The same drama as four years ago takes place. There are harsh words in the men's meetings, insincere apologies, flower missions. I have increasingly desperate phone calls with Gina in Amsterdam. First she tries to help me with the feedback that I receive from the others, but later she joins in and gives me her own increasingly strong feedback.

Eventually I am once again expelled from the Sangha. My relationship with Gina, our spiritual partnership, is automatically null and void. Relationships between students at different levels are not allowed. My relationship with Gina only existed by Andrew's grace, and now I have fallen from grace.

I am destroyed over the loss of Gina. If Andrew hadn't sent her to Amsterdam none of this would have happened. All the intimacy and the trust, has that suddenly gone? All the love, has it suddenly gone too? What kind of spiritual revolution is it, when two people who love each other can't be together? Who does he think he is to stick his head in my love life? Can't Gina and I decide for ourselves whether we love each other or not? But Gina is far away in Amsterdam, and she has turned her back on me, disgusted by my weakness. Deep down, I'm still convinced she loves me, and is only mouthing the party line. But she's so hard and cold now. Is she protecting herself from her love for me, a love the community no longer wishes her to feel? Or am I just a deluded romantic fool?

I go and live in an apartment nearby. I am more furious with Andrew now than ever. I ask myself: Why don't I just leave? Haven't seven years of suffering been enough? But leaving Andrew would mean leaving Gina. And I'm still in love with her. To regain Gina's respect I will have to make it back into Andrew's community. So I cling to every inch of conviction that is still left in me.

Apart from Gina, my inner conflict about Andrew rages unabatedly. My soul is coming up empty, and I beat myself up for that. Then something unexpected happens.

On a teaching trip in New York City, Andrew and his wife are run over by a cab driving through a red light. Andrew's arm is broken, but he could just as well have been killed. Alka suffers a bad concussion and a fractured jaw.

The news sends shock waves through the community. That night I'm afraid to fall asleep, out of fear I'll have a heart attack and won't wake up. The possibility of Andrew being taken away from me has brought out my terror of death. I realize that Andrew is still deep in my cells, no matter what. He is my lifeline, my connection with the divine. No amount of anger or doubt could ever change that. This realization energizes me and puts me back in the perspective. All is not lost. I just have to recover ground, find my way past the negative emotions. I'm like a horse that faltered in jumping a hurdle and must regroup to have another go at it. I move in with three other students who have also fallen from grace, and together we try to make it back into the community.

* * *

It is November 1994. Four of us sit in the living room together, in our apartment in Mill Valley: Jose, the Spanish dancer who now makes a living as a window cleaner; Donald, the young American from Long Island, also a window cleaner; Ron, a forty-year-old American carpenter; and me. Four tired soldiers that had to leave the front for a while. We were all prominent community members; we had a lot to say in the men's meetings. And all of us have fallen from our pedestals.

Jose and Donald are both plucking guitars. Ron is playing around on a keyboard. I'm behind my computer. Then Jose comes up with a new composition. On a few simple chords he sings:

Doesn't matter what you think
Doesn't matter what you feel
Only matters what you do

A true soldier's song! We all join in. That refrain sums up Andrew's teaching. It sums up the mission that we have to fulfill. No matter what we think, however many doubts we have, no matter how rotten we feel, however much resistance or unwillingness, it only matters that we 'do it'. One thing that keeps us going is the impersonal perspective. Everybody falls sooner or later, it just happens to be our turn now. Unlike John we are lucky enough to get a second or third chance. We're all fighting the same epic battle, nameless players in the age-old fight of good against evil. We may not be winning the battle at the moment, but at least we are fighting.

And yet the four of us are actually having a good time. Part of us enjoys living under less pressure. No Sangha meetings to go through; not having to 'respond' all the time, not having to wave the flag for enlightenment. Still, we inch towards more pressure. We give each other feedback when we see each other being sloppy, dishonest, or hanging back too much. And the minute you give someone else feedback you are maintaining some kind of standard, so you have to hold yourself to that standard as well.

Before we know it we're living as if it is a Sangha house. We have regular house meetings. We do voluntary community service. I transcribe Andrew's dialogs and wash dishes in the community restaurant. We go to satsang and are inspired by Andrew's teachings. In a few months, we change from washed-out losers to inspired students, desperately wanting to be readmitted into Andrew's field of grace.

In January 1995, in Bodh Gaya, I meet up with Gina for the first time since last summer. There have been some uneasy phone conversations between us, and some email exchanges in which I try to prove to her that something is changing for me. Now she sits down with me and tells me in no uncertain terms that I have to stop holding on to the past.

"It's finished between us." She says, "What we had together is gone. You've thrown it all away by being so stubborn and proud. But I see that you're trying to make it back as Andrew's student. That's very good. We can still be good friends as students of Andrew, and once you're back into the community it will be appropriate for us to have more contact again. But now you really have to let go of your attachment to me."

I look at her with a begging expression in my eyes.

"But don't you feel anything for me anymore?" I ask her. "The love, the intimacy, do you still feel it?"

"Of course I feel a lot of love for you," she says, "but that is impersonal. There's nothing special about it. Your insistence that there'd be something special between us is exactly what's gotten you into trouble. You have to stop being so sentimental."

I nod. I feel I'd rather be dead at this moment, but I try to be understanding and impersonal.

"I'm happy we talked," Gina says, "and that things are much clearer between us now. I hope you make it back as a formal student."

I'm heartbroken. This is not the Gina that I knew. Or is she right, and am I just holding on to sentimental memories? After she's walked out of the room, I sit and cry for a long time.

A week later I apply to be readmitted as a formal student. I speak to one of the senior students and manage to convince him that something has really changed for me, that I'm ready to go for it again. Andrew fulfills my request. People congratulate me, Gina too. But Andrew makes it clear that he has even less faith in me now than after my last crisis. When I thank him for my renewed admission into the community, he only says, "Actions speak louder than words."

6

FOR THE SAKE OF THE WHOLE

The whole point of spiritual experience is evolution. That evolution occurs, and the true significance of human life is found, when we cease to live for ourselves but live only for the sake of the whole.

-Andrew Cohen

6.1. Still Looking for Leaders

When we return from the Bodh Gaya retreat, I move into a formal student house. Shortly afterwards my three buddies also make it back as formal students. We notice that the stakes have gone up. Impersonal enlightenment has to transform our lives; we should banish any trace of a personal life. Our very reason for living should be dedicated to what Andrew calls 'living for the sake of the whole'.

In Marin the Sangha has now been split, under Andrew's guidance, into about ten committed students and eighty formal students. The committed students live with Andrew and are groomed for leadership in Europe, where the revolution seems to be taking off at last. The

London center grows to about 40 formal students, the Amsterdam center to about 15. They are led by committed students from the Marin Sangha who have moved to Europe. There's talk of setting up centers in Germany, in Tel Aviv, in Sydney. The time for sitting in satsang in our self-absorbed "Marin bubble" has passed. It's time to go beyond ourselves now, time for action: go out into the world, establish centers, organize talks, video showings, meditation evenings, translate Andrew's books, spread Andrew's message, while throughout being a shining example of his teachings.

On his yearly teaching trips to Israel Andrew has met with several well-known rabbis, and he becomes inspired by them as he was by the Tibetan Buddhist lamas before in Bodh Gaya. Even though Andrew is Jewish, he was not raised with Jewish traditions. Yet his teachings now seem to become more Jewish than Buddhist. It's more important to do the right thing than to have some profound inner experience of enlightenment. Andrew speaks about creating heaven on earth. The Sangha should be a beacon of light in a dark and ignorant world—a laboratory and showcase of enlightened living, living without personal agenda. As long as at least some people will live justly and with integrity, there's still hope for the world.

So in this way, ethics becomes more important than metaphysics or mysticism, just like in the Jewish teachings we can only serve God by obeying his laws. God is hiding in his creation, and by observing the laws of the Torah we can make him manifest and create heaven on earth. Has Andrew travelled from psychoanalysis to Advaita

Vedanta to Tibetan Buddhism to finally come home to his native Jewish faith?

Andrew speaks repeatedly about his need for more committed students and more leaders. Those who've been with him for many years would be especially suited for such a role. In a Sangha meeting Andrew appeals to his long-term students, most of whom have one or more crises behind them, to rise up and become "heavy players." In my case, that means going to Amsterdam. In April, Gina visits Marin for a week. She and Harry are still leading the center in Amsterdam, now joined by Harry's girlfriend Sophia. She'd been in a similar position as me last year, but she had pulled through. It's ironic. My best friend and my ex-girlfriend are leading the center in my hometown, and I'm not allowed to join them there. Gina is now a big shot; she stays in Andrew's house in San Anselmo and has the privilege of being his personal attendant for the week. I meet her for coffee, but just as in Bodh Gaya I find it difficult to feel the old intimacy between us. I find her cold and hard. She clearly feels that she's made it and, although I've become a formal student, I'm still of a lower echelon.

In June I put in a request with Andrew to be allowed to move to the Amsterdam center. At first Andrew seems fairly positive about it. But then there is a problem. I did not check with Harry and Gina before I put in my request to Andrew. I'm still a solo player, not a team player. Therefore, Andrew decides against it. He feels I've been trying to impose my presence in Amsterdam on Harry and Gina, motivated by secretly wanting to get back together with Gina. So I'm grounded in Marin. I'm not ready yet.

One of the older students who do respond to Andrew's call is my buddy Jose. In the men's meeting he takes up a leader's role, he initiates things, and proves he would be well suited to be a committed student. Andrew is visibly impressed by Jose's progress. During a men's outing with Andrew to San Francisco, which Jose organized, they are talking together like two lovers. In August 1995, Andrew asks Jose to be a committed student. But he tells him that he has to be ready. He has to be willing "rather to be burned alive than betray Andrew." Jose agrees, and speaks movingly in the men's meeting about his unconditional dedication to Andrew's teachings, his willingness to face anything that might come up for him in this new situation and make increased demands on him. We all congratulate Jose on his rapid ascension through the ranks. From outcast to committed student in eight months—so it is possible to rise up in the face of adversity!

In October we celebrate Andrew's fortieth birthday. It is a big event. We rent a hall in Sausalito, have a six-course dinner, and prepare acts to be performed for Andrew. Jose organizes a men's group recital of one of Andrew's excerpts describing his new view of bringing Heaven to Earth. Each man recites one line, and Jose arranges the whole into an impressive performance. The last line is loudly and triumphantly recited in unison. Andrew is pleased, especially with Jose. We hear that Jose will go to Germany to lead the center there.

A month later we hear the news: Jose has left the community.

In a men's meeting a few days later one of the committed students tells us what happened. "Jose just wasn't willing to face himself," he says. "He was great at giving others feedback but wasn't willing to look at himself." As is the case with everyone who leaves, Jose is viewed with scorn and contempt. He hadn't the courage to face himself.

I am shaken and dejected by the news. It hits close to home. A close brother has died in battle. My cynicism deepens. Didn't Andrew make Jose a committed student too soon? Didn't he make an error of judgment? In a Sangha meeting a month later Andrew admits as much. "Robert didn't feel he was ready yet, but I really needed him for Germany. So I thought it was worth giving him a shot." Andrew seems philosophical about it. You win some, you lose some. His viewpoint on such matters expresses no concern for the plight of the individual—the success of the teachings is all that matters.

Much later I hear that Jose had decided he'd had enough of the humiliation and verbal battering. He knew it was only going to get worse, and that he would only get through by giving in and telling his interrogators what they wanted to hear. Just a year prior, he'd been in a similar situation in Amsterdam. He'd decided to pack his bags and leave. But after announcing to Harry what he was going to do, Harry and Andrew had managed to talk him back into staying. To avoid a similar situation, he packed his bags in the middle of the night and left, without saying anything to anyone—the end of an eight-year long involvement with Andrew.

During this time, the issue of money becomes an urgent one in the community. Many students are strapped financially. They have built up huge debts traveling to

India and Europe with Andrew. Since most of us don't have college degrees, career prospects are dim. Also, the community schedule doesn't allow much time for career building. Andrew criticizes us for avoiding the issue of money and for not taking responsibility for our finances. He wants us to take a stand and get it together financially. Exactly how this is to be done, he leaves up to us. We set up regular "money meetings" where we address those students who are most in debt, and put pressure on them to get their act together. We make wild plans for setting up community businesses. I start a web site design business called MaxWeb Designs with three other students. For about half a year we try to get it going, but it takes too much time and energy to combine it with all the community obligations. In the end, all four of us return to our jobs that at least give us a dependable income.

In August there is more news from the front. Gina falls from her pedestal in Amsterdam. Apparently she's become proud and arrogant, and now she's in the same mess as I was before. She is sent back to Marin and now it's she who is in the doghouse. When I meet her she looks crestfallen and discouraged. She's thinking about leaving altogether. She apologizes for being so hard with me, says she was on a big ego trip. I don't know what to say. Why do we treat each other so horribly as Andrew's students? Is that the result of spiritual evolution? It makes me angry.

Andrew says that Gina's self-confidence was based all along on ambition, and not on an impersonal passion to serve the revolution. Gina's crisis echoes my own experiences with editing the book. My old friend Doubt is having a field day. Isn't this a general pattern between

Andrew and his students? First he praises you, gives you more responsibility, and makes you feel you're his chosen disciple. You work sixteen hours a day serving the revolution. Inevitably your ego gets inflated because you occupy a star position. When that comes to light, Andrew is shocked by your monstrous egocentricity, turns his back on you disgustedly, and feels betrayed by yet another student.

* * * *

Meanwhile Andrew continues to push for more sexual relationships within the community. He feels that sexuality is still being avoided. During a teaching trip to the East Coast Andrew gives us an ultimatum: he will only return to Marin if there are three new sexual relationships. Within three days there are three new relationships in the community. But the unspoken demand for more relationships lingers. In December 1995, I am asked to be in a relationship by Marianne, a German housemate of mine. She has been around for seven years, I for eight. We are both seasoned veterans, with a similar background as far as romance is concerned. She has been in a Sangha relationship in which she got very romantically attached. When Andrew broke up the relationship she had a hard time getting over her attachment. Andrew feels it would be good for her to be in another more 'impersonal' relationship in order to get over her romantic ideals. People feel it's also good for me to get over my romantic attachment to Gina, so Marianne and I seem to be well-matched.

I happen to know that she was actually more attracted to Jose, and had asked Andrew to be in a relationship with him. Andrew had said no. Being second choice doesn't bother me that much. As my housemate she's been privy to my yearnings for the lost relationship with Gina, and my continued romantic feelings for her. So, although I like Marianne a lot, she must realize she's also second choice for me. A good basis for an 'impersonal' relationship: I am not in love, neither is she.

Once again I am torn between my personal preference and 'the right thing to do.' Since Gina has returned from Amsterdam a few months ago in a mess, we have talked a few times. Obviously a relationship between us is out of the question now. She is an outcast and I'm a formal student. Would I want to wait until Gina is doing better and try to be with her again? But of course Andrew would never allow it. I get together with a friend in the community and we talk about it openly. Do I want to hang on to my romantic feelings for Gina, she asks me, or is it something I want to take a stand against? What is my bottom line? Just like so many times before, I decide to go by what I feel is the deeper truth of the situation according to Andrew's teaching. So I say yes to Marianne.

We get together and go on a two-day honeymoon to an expensive hotel in Oakland. It's a part time honeymoon, on both days Marianne has to work in the community café. What a stark contrast to my honeymoon with Gina two and a half years ago. I don't mind. I don't want to be hurt as badly as I was with Gina. The sex works out well between us, and we seem to be compatible—the perfect relationship according to the teachings. Now that any possible hidden agenda about Gina has been eliminated, Andrew grants my longstanding wish to go to Amsterdam. Two weeks after Marianne and I get together, Andrew asks both of us to move to Amsterdam to help develop the community there. After eight years in the States, I want to get out of Marin where things feel more and more stale, and move to Europe, the new epicenter of Andrew's revolution. Within a week I pack my things and move to Amsterdam. Marianne still has to work and will come a month later.

6.2. On a Mission in Amsterdam

When I arrive in Amsterdam I notice the community there seems beaten down. A month ago Andrew was here for his semi-annual visit, and the community members made an unforgivable mistake. It happened during a dinner with Andrew in an Indonesian restaurant. Such dinners with Andrew are a rare opportunity these days. It's not like the early years, when you could just invite Andrew over. And as thrilling and wonderful as those meetings with Andrew are, they are also quite stressful. Everything is formal and has to be arranged perfectly, and everyone has to be on their best behavior.

That evening everyone was waiting in the restaurant, filled with tense anticipation. Andrew was late, fifteen minutes, half an hour, forty-five minutes. That's not unusual. Andrew runs on his own time, and often has unexpected telephone calls or spontaneous impulses that make him lose sight of the time. Harry, who was with Andrew, telephoned the restaurant. His message seemed to indicate that it was all right to start eating, that Andrew wouldn't arrive for a while. Relieved, everyone did so. This turned out to be a fatal mistake. When Andrew eventually entered the restaurant with Harry, he was furious about this lack of respect.

A few days later, in January 1996, there is the annual retreat in Bodh Gaya. I travel there with my Amsterdam buddies. But for the Dutch students this retreat is no fun. Andrew is still upset with them. When he feels they're not fully responding to him, and not taking their transgression seriously, he asks Albert to have a meeting with them. Albert is a Dutchman, a committed student now in charge of the center in Germany. Andrew asks me to assist Albert. This is a good opportunity for me to practice leadership skills. The purpose of the meeting is to bring the Dutch students to a greater sense of urgency, to shake them out of their passivity and lethargy, so they can respond appropriately and change. That they are in such a crisis, Andrew partly attributes to their cultural conditioning. He says the Germans are conditioned to be heavy and morbid; the English are conditioned to be emotionally reserved and cut off. The Dutch, he feels, are too informal and casual, and the restaurant incident is an inexcusable example of that.

* * *

We're sitting in one of the bedrooms of the Tourist Bungalow, the building complex where the formal students live. All the Amsterdam students, about ten of them, plus Albert and me, are gathered in a circle. Albert explains why we are having this meeting. Andrew is still deeply insulted by the restaurant incident. The Dutch haven't responded adequately, they've hardly apologized, according to Andrew. He feels the Dutch are very rude and impolite, with no sense of etiquette and interpersonal manners.

Albert says, "Guys, we're Dutch amongst each other, and I have to tell you, I'm almost ashamed to be Dutch. What you've done to Andrew is completely outrageous. What were you thinking for God's sake?"

A few Dutch students answer guiltily, like dogs with their tails between their legs. They mumble excuses and promise to do better.

"Guys, you just can't do this. What are you planning to do? I feel you're not taking responsibility for what you've done. And you're not really changing. When you arrived in Bodh Gaya, you didn't even say hello to Robert. He felt very hurt by that. Are you actually intending to change?"

More stammered answers, psychological explanations. It is obvious that the Dutch students don't know how to answer.

I take my chance to put in my two cents.

"It's not about what kind of psychological insights you have about yourself," I say severely. "Do you want to change, yes or no? What is your intention? I don't feel your clarity of intention."

Well, that one landed. Albert looks at me approvingly. The Dutch feel even more uncomfortable now, which is exactly the idea.

But Doubt whispers: "What is this lack of clarity of intention that they've manifested? Not putting enlightenment first under all circumstances? Or not putting Andrew first under all circumstances?"

Next Albert addresses the Dutch students one by one, goes extensively into their personal shortcomings, and gives them a rough verbal shakeup. Once in a while I butt in with a strong remark. After an hour the Dutch students are desperate. They promise they will do better and will make a big gesture to Andrew, to convince him that they mean it. Some of them are on the verge of tears.

Afterwards Albert pulls me aside with a concerned look on his face. "Was I too hard?" he asks. I am moved by his humility. "No, Albert," I say, "you were very good. You brought them exactly to that point of urgency where they have to be. You put them in touch with their clarity of intention." Reassured Albert goes off to Andrew to report on his mission.

* * *

Finally, by way of some response, the Dutch students offer to organize and manage the traditional final party of the Bodh Gaya retreat. That is a nice gesture but not completely sufficient. Andrew tells them to get some etiquette lessons, to learn some manners. After the retreat, back in Amsterdam, the students contact an etiquette teacher and have a weekly session with her for ten weeks. The last session consists of going to a restaurant together, using the correct knives and forks, following the right protocol, saying the right things. It is a humiliating process, from which Marianne and I are luckily exempted.

In Amsterdam I throw myself into my new job full of inspiration. I am more or less Harry's right hand man, his lieutenant. Harry and Sophia now lead the center. There are about fifteen formal students, and about the same number of less involved lay students. The students in Amsterdam are enthusiastic, but don't have as much experience with Andrew's teachings. One of the things that Marianne and I should bring to the community is an example of what it means to take a firm stand with each other.

Harry and Sophia ask me to take a stand with my housemate Erica, a single mother with an eight-year old daughter. Erica is not taking responsibility for her finances, they say. She has large debts. So now I'm having a meeting with her once a week, in which Erica shows me all her bank statements and her bills. I find out pretty soon that it's a simple situation. More money is going out than is coming in. As we go through it I'm struck with the stark reality of her situation. It's not possible for her to make ends meet and to meet all her community obligations at the same time. I suggest to Harry that maybe Erica shouldn't go to the summer retreat in Switzerland. But Harry shakes his head. That's not an option. Andrew has already said that he wants all the Europeans to come, with no exceptions.

I feel torn. Erica is squeezed from all sides. She's broke and she can't spend enough time with her daughter. From Andrew's perspective, she's behaving like a victim and she should just go for it and push through. As a loyal student I put a lot of pressure on Erica to get her finances together, but privately I feel it would be better if she was allowed time off from community activities to be able to make money.

After a while the pressure becomes too much for Erica. She breaks down and says she doesn't want to be a student anymore. I speak to Harry and Sophia about it and we agree it's the best thing for Erica to step down as a student and be involved in a more casual way with the community. But when Harry tells Andrew the news, Andrew refuses to take no for an answer. He calls Erica and tells her she's deluded and he doesn't agree. He feels she just wants to run away from the pressure. He wants her to push through. Erica decides to stay on, and a few months later she even shaves her head and becomes celibate. Andrew can be persuasive. But it doesn't feel right to me. It just doesn't feel right.

In the summer of 1996, we have the annual European retreat in Switzerland. It begins as a beautiful time. On a high mountaintop, three hundred people live for two weeks together. Andrew gives talks in a large tent twice a day. For two weeks there is nothing else to do but be immersed in the teachings of enlightenment. In the early mornings, I go running along the mountain paths with Robert and the other committed students. I am completely happy in these moments. If only life could always be like this.

We increasingly hear about a new development in Andrew's teaching. Andrew has summarized his teaching into five theses he calls 'the five fundamentals', and all of us must study and contemplate these theses thoroughly. The theses all sound familiar:

> Clarity of intention is the foundation of spiritual life
> Volitionality: it is within our power to change

We have to face everything and avoid nothing

Impersonality: there is nothing personal about any of our experiences

Living for the sake of the whole is the essence of the spiritual life

Andrew says that these five fundamentals should become our new psychology, the way in which we interpret all of our experience. This is the new way to think. In this way, Andrew wants to bring about a deep transformation in our thinking and feeling. The five fundamentals are discussed nonstop in our men's and women's meetings and expounded by Andrew in public teachings and meetings with his students. If we want to speak about personal matters, we can only do so in the context of the five fundamentals. During the meditation retreats in India and Switzerland we're no longer allowed to have any personal conversations, only conversations about the five fundamentals.

I'm not sure what to think of this new development. It sounds like Andrew is systematizing his teaching, something I was convinced he would never do. Andrew always made fun of organized religion; he said it was the death of any living spirituality. To me it feels suffocating. It often feels artificial to fit my whole experience into these tenets. However, the truth of this dogma is not to be doubted publicly. In the early years Andrew had always encouraged free inquiry. Now it seems Andrew has determined all the answers, and where our inquiries should lead — to the truth of the five fundamentals. Has he become allergic to doubt?

Slowly but surely the community moves in a more 'impersonal' direction. Speaking about personal problems, personal interests, or ourselves is not considered helpful. Attention to 'our personal drama' is discouraged. Independent thinking outside the perimeters of Andrew's teaching becomes suspect. Why would you want to inquire into anything outside the five fundamentals when the five fundamentals are all that you need to focus on in order to realize freedom? Investigation into truth is still highly valued, but the perimeters of that investigation are now clearly defined.

Doubt has its own take on this. Hasn't the community become more and more self-focused, even incestuous? Sometimes I feel like a monk tucked away in some monastic order, while the rest of the world is moving on. To conquer Doubt, I tell myself that we're the carriers of a precious spiritual teaching that is too subtle and too demanding for the world at large to accept. We're the pockets of light in a barren world, the trees that give oxygen to the rest of humanity, by committing ourselves to transformation, to Andrew's teaching—so desperately needed by the world today but still unrecognized. I tell myself that this is what it means to live for the sake of the whole. Doubt listens with mock respect.

* * *

It's Thursday afternoon January 21, 1997. Andrew, Harry and I walk through the Staalstraat in Amsterdam. We're on our way to a public event featuring Andrew. It's been a long time since I've had much personal contact with him. These days he seems very remote, very different from 1989 when I worked with John on the book or those early days in Devon. But during this visit to Amsterdam I have a chance to see him more often. He is staying with Harry and Sophia in their flat in the Rozenstraat and I am invited over a few times. Andrew shows me articles for the upcoming Journal, proudly shows me a letter from Ken Wilber, it is almost like the old days. Yet again I am privy to some of the goings on in the inner circle. There's a reason for all this personal attention from Andrew. With the help of my old philosophy professor I've organized a public lecture at the University of Amsterdam under the title "Each his own Truth? On the postmodern fear of the Absolute." Andrew approved the title after much deliberation, and I have briefed him on postmodernism. Andrew thinks the lecture could be a good inroad to the academic circuit, and will hopefully garner some publicity.

The lecture goes well. The room is full of philosophy students eager to hear Andrew present his teachings. A reporter from the Dutch newspaper Trouw is there. I feel as if my rating has improved a few notches. For a change I'm advancing Andrew's cause rather than just being a nuisance to him and not meeting his expectations.

Two days later the newspaper article appears in the Trouw. It is mostly positive and good PR for Andrew. Only the last paragraph seems to contain some irony. It mentions the fact that Andrew has his students shave their heads, but that his own hairdo is perfectly coiffed.

Harry, Andrew and I are sitting at the kitchen table in the Rozenstraat when Harry reads the article to Andrew in

English. Andrew shows no response until those last lines. Then he pulls a face.

"What a bastard, that interviewer. He seemed like such a nice guy. Call him up Harry! Tell him he's a jerk."

"Well, Andrew, that's maybe not such a good idea…"

"What? Don't you dare? Or do you agree with him?"

"No, of course it's ridiculous what he writes. But maybe we should keep the relationship with him intact."

"He's an incompetent journalist. Then just tell him he's no good at his profession."

Harry tries in all possible ways to be spared this hit job. He is the leader of the center in Amsterdam and has to live with its consequences. In the end, Andrew lets the matter rest.

6.3. Doubt Versus the Mystery

A few weeks later we're off to India again. The annual retreat in India is no longer held in the filthy village of Bodh Gaya, where surrounded by dirt and bacteria, many people got very sick over the years. Now we fly five hours to Delhi, then travel five hours on the train north to Rishikesh, a friendly town where the air is still clean, in the foothills of the Himalayas. Rishikesh means "city of saints" and lies near the source of the holy river Ganges. There are more ashrams, sadhus, ascetics, and prophets per square foot than anywhere else in India. We've rented an ashram for two weeks, where the retreat will take place. It's a walled-in complex, with the Indian variant of condominiums in it. Compared to the poverty and squalor of Bodh Gaya, this is like a luxurious winter resort. The pleasant winter sun contributes to this impression.

The talks and meditations take place in a big hall in the center of the ashram. Andrew sits cross-legged on a small platform, and 275 people sit in a U-shape around him, most of them cross-legged on the floor and some on chairs against the wall. Andrew gives meditation instructions, and speaks about the importance of daily practice, necessary to break the accumulated flow of built up karma, the enormous momentum of the need to see ourselves as separate individuals. He says we don't know what our destiny will be, whether it's full enlightenment or something very short of that. But the result doesn't matter. As long as we totally dedicate ourselves to the spiritual path, we are free. All we can do is purify ourselves with full commitment; the rest is up to our karma and grace.

It's a relief to no longer have to comply with an impossible demand of being perfectly enlightened (whatever that may mean). But it's confusing that now the process of purification is all that matters, that it has become a goal in and of itself. Doubt and I have some challenging conversations. What happened to enlightenment then? Was Andrew wrong when he said we were all enlightened in the beginning? Or did we prove him wrong by continuing to have egos? And what is so revolutionary about his message now? Isn't he now teaching himself what he accused the Buddhist teachers of back in 1987? Just walk the path and don't bother about enlightenment?

"Look at the dignity and honor of a life that is not for yourself," Andrew says. "Care for the whole is not a personal decision. It's a deeply felt evolutionary impulse that is screaming, 'this must happen!' We have to respond to this from the depth of our conscience."

Doubt pipes up again. "Are you sure it's an evolutionary impulse that's screaming at you or is it simply Andrew who's screaming at you?"

The shared meditations are immediately very powerful. I write in my diary: Felt in the room one current, one flow, one Mystery pulsating—almost visually vibrant. The room seemed to be constantly imploding upon itself. 275 people struck one beautiful chord together. It felt like tipping my toe into a vast overwhelming Reality—the way things always are and have been and will be; a glimpse of how glorious life can be; a resonant vibrant expression of this Mystery.

The next day I share my ecstatic experience with Andrew during a community meeting with him.

"The experience was the same as ten years ago," I say, with too much excitement.

"Did you think it would have changed then?" Andrew says. "The Mystery is always there, whether we're in contact with it or not."

He looks at me with some surprise in his eyes, as if he wants to say, "How can you after ten years still be raving about the Mystery. You've been experiencing it for ten years now, probably hundreds of times. Why so excited about old news? Why act as if it's all new?"

He's right of course. But he doesn't know about Doubt. Realizing we're talking at cross-purposes, I try to continue the conversation.

"I recognize the need for daily practice. Because of the intensive meditations during retreats like this one, I become very much in touch again with that Mystery, but after the retreat that fades away, in the midst of the pressures of ordinary daily life."

It's a cautious reference to the seemingly hopeless battle in Amsterdam, the struggle to combine the demands of daily life with Andrew's demands for spiritual practice. I think about Erica's predicament with money and her daughter.

"Ordinary daily life?" Andrew frowns. "Our daily life is anything but ordinary. That's a wrong way of looking at it. And as my student you should never allow yourself to let that Mystery fade away so much. I give you all the tools necessary to stay in touch with that Mystery."

Oops. I guess it's not a topic for discussion. I struggle to regain my bearings. I manage to say, "Yes, the tools are very helpful. My practice of running five miles a day gives me self-confidence, strength, puts me more deeply in touch with my intention to be free."

"You're a fast runner," Andrew says, "I heard you did something nasty this morning. You were running with Robert when you suddenly started racing him without warning."

Everyone laughs, Andrew too. It's a playful hint at my competitive nature. I'm relieved this conversation has been brought to a successful end. But actually this little dialog says a lot about how much my relationship with him has changed over the years. In the beginning it was effortless; I felt intimacy, love, and passion. Now it feels like I'm just trying to please him, trying to prove something, show myself to be a good student. With a shock I realize that I'm actually afraid of him. I've experienced too often how he holds my fate in his hands, and that staying on his good side is crucial for survival.

Andrew has a new surprise for his men students. Physical strength and endurance have always fascinated him. He himself has been practicing three hours of yoga every day for years. Now he's thought up something new for the men: pushups. One morning before breakfast we all stand on the roof of one of the buildings of the ashrams, in sports gear. The idea is to do as many pushups as possible, without knees touching the floor. I am fairly athletic by nature, but this is not fun. Not participating is not an option. Eventually, with a lot of resting on my hands, I manage to do a hundred pushups. Others, who have done this more often, manage to do as many as three hundred. Andrew comes by to watch and to encourage us. He thinks it's great that the men are doing this. He himself doesn't join in; he has a chronic arm injury, from the taxi accident in New York City. The push-ups now become a weekly ritual. Everyone is meant to participate. Be there or be square. Many of us get minor injuries.

Back in Amsterdam we do a pushup marathon every Sunday—literally, do pushups until we drop. Pretty soon we are standing on our hands for three to five hours, doing pushups in series of ten. Some of us manage to do thousands of pushups; the record is ten thousand. This becomes too time-consuming, therefore the rules are changed: do as many pushups as you can in an hour's time. You are supposed to break your record every week. At a certain point one of my fellow Dutch students expresses his frustration with this senseless undertaking. When Andrew hears about it, he sends him a message: he shouldn't behave like a baby. The incident seems to strengthen Andrew's conviction that Dutch men are wimps. I also find the pushup marathon a ridiculous and meaningless undertaking. But I think twice before saying that out loud. These are the rules of the game, and this is how it is played. Although I could do without these macho performances, in all fairness it has to be said that some of the other guys love it. They gain a lot of self-confidence from it, even more so because of the attention and respect they're getting from Andrew.

6.4. The Mission Turns Sour

After the 1997 Rishikesh retreat, the Mystery is drowned pretty quickly again in the midst of community life, which becomes increasingly black and white, a cosmic battle of good versus evil. We talk about facing and uprooting archetypical layers of conditioning that have been in place for years. The minimum amount of spiritual practice in the community increases to three hours a day. Every Sunday there is a four-hour communal meditation session, followed in the afternoon by a pushup marathon. Because of the cosmic proportions of Andrew's undertaking, no holds are barred when it comes to breaking through our conditioning.

Andrew wants us to keep a diary in which we write about our daily experience in the light of the five fundamentals. I write about how we are not separate from the whole, how we have to respond to life without self-preoccupation, and so on. From the diary it becomes clear what our mindset is: we have to dedicate our lives to burning up karma. What else is there to do? How could it ever be conceivable to go back to a personal life? Again and again the question comes back: are we living for ourselves or are we living for others? It's one way or the other. I write in my diary, "without the impersonal perspective none of this makes any sense, and with the impersonal perspective nothing else makes sense." Doubt says, "The diary is actually more like continuous pep talk than genuine self-exploration."

Marianne and I become prominent students, but we don't quite become the leaders that everybody wants us to be. I am criticized for not giving enough, keeping my own life going, and thinking of myself instead of giving to the whole. In my diary I write a lot about "just keeping going," "hanging in there," as if these have now become virtues. It is a stark contrast with the "we are already enlightened here and now" jubilation from ten years ago. Others point out to me the gap between what I experientially know (my glorious experiences of the Mystery) and what I actually live up to. I have to respond more, give more, engage more, be more interested, and take more risks. Again and again I berate myself for not having changed that much over the past ten years. I feel guilty and fraudulent. So I work very hard, try to give even more, deny myself free time and personal enjoyments. I'm endlessly doing battle with what I feel must be my emotional weakness and my selfishness.

In the summer of 1997, there is a bit more room for joy. Andrew comes to visit, he gives public teachings, and we have a nice outing to the beach with him. In August there is the annual summer retreat in Switzerland, where there are long hours of meditation and the Mystery can again reign supreme.

When I come back from Switzerland, I hear that my buddy Donald has left. That's the second of the four soldiers who's thrown in the towel. But I don't have time to reflect on this very much. Sophia falls from grace and is sent to America to do a retreat. I can see it's very painful for Harry, that he misses her. As long-time students, Marianne and I are expected to take more responsibility in running the center now that Sophia has gone. Sophia was a wizard at organizing things and keeping a community up and running.

Meanwhile, back in the States, Andrew has found a new international home base for his community, a country estate called Foxhollow in the Berkshires of Massachusetts. For two million dollars, he buys the estate which includes a mansion and several condominiums, surrounded by rolling hills, towering pines and breathtaking views of the countryside. This is to be the new ashram. Clearly all of Andrew's students in Marin are expected to move to the new headquarters. But at the same time, Andrew feels that his students take it for granted that they can move to such a beautiful ashram. He demands a display of loyalty and commitment from them. Each student has to pay money to be allowed to live there:

a thousand dollars for each year that they've been involved with Andrew, with a maximum of five thousand dollars. The money is a problem for many students who are already struggling with financial issues. Nonetheless, by the end of 1996, the bulk of the community has moved from Marin to Foxhollow.

In October 1997, I visit Foxhollow for ten days. It is a beautiful and expansive estate. In the centrally located mansion, meditations, video showings, and meals take place. Everyone lives together in the surrounding condos. On my first day in Foxhollow I see Andrew standing in the hall, after the lunch period, talking to some people. He looks my way, our eyes meet, and I feel a hesitation, shyness. What should I do? Go up to him? Wave? What are the regulations for a situation like this? He breaks the short impasse and says, "Don't be such a weirdo and come and greet me." I feel embarrassed. Hastily I walk towards him and embrace him. I feel no intimacy.

I also meet my old friend and foe John again. After his departure in 1994, he has repeatedly begged Andrew to be allowed back. Andrew finally consented, and John lives now as a formal student in Foxhollow. But to me, since last I saw him, he's become a shadow of his former self, a shell of a person. I am sorry to see him in this condition.

I spend a lot of time with Patrick, a formal student from the London community. Both Patrick and I are training to run a marathon. During our long running sessions we talk a lot. Recently, the English men's group has been summoned to Foxhollow because they are in a crisis. They are not tough enough on each other in the men's meetings. The Foxhollow men show them how not to give each other's egos any room. Some Englishmen have been stubborn in the meetings. Patrick was one of them, and that's why he has stayed on in Foxhollow after the others have returned to England. Patrick tells me how he didn't take a stand in one of the meetings, so afterwards he was physically roughed up by a few men, and how that has helped him. "They forced me to get in touch with my own fighting spirit," he says, "and go beyond my apathy." He says that now he understands what it really means to be a man.

I try to hide my alarm. I find it repelling to hear about such physical abuse. "Why are you shocked?" says Doubt. "Isn't it the logical consequence of the verbal beatings that have been common for so long? It's the next step. In love and war everything is allowed." I force myself to shut up this inner voice and put my attention on the conversation. Patrick tells me that another Englishman had a similar treatment but protested and didn't cooperate. The next day he was no longer a formal student.

Patrick and I speak about the European centers. By now it's become very clear that the revolution in Europe is not happening — hardly any new people are coming. We both feel that the students there are overworked; there are too few people, everyone lives crunched together in houses which are too small, gets too little sleep and has money problems all the time. Why does Andrew need to create this revolution in Europe? Why not just make Foxhollow a kind of monastery where students could dedicate themselves to his teachings, and have a few minimal satellite centers in Europe? Such thoughts are not popular. They reek of doubt about Andrew's mission. They would suggest that in the midst of a community dedicated to facing everything and avoiding nothing, perhaps not that much is faced and a lot is avoided. Are we only facing what Andrew wants us to face? Is it ever possible to discuss whether Andrew is avoiding anything? Issues of work and money for example? Or power relations between him and his students, students being beaten into submission?

6.5. Rishikesh 1998: The Women's Conditioning

Andrew has always seemed skeptical of women's ability to live his teachings. In 1989, he started to talk about a deeply rooted resistance in women that was not present in men. In 1992, Andrew began to espouse a theory about 'women's conditioning'. According to Andrew, due to millennia of deeply rooted conditioning, women have an engrained survival instinct that prevents them from truly letting go of the personal and embracing the impersonal perspective. Andrew's women students are considered inferior to the men, not able to meet together in the impersonal view like the men. At least that is how it seems to me. In 1997, Andrew starts to put increasing pressure on his women students. He feels they're not objective enough, too emotional, and too personal. It starts out with what seems to be some marital strife with his wife Alka. He feels she's not surrendering to him. Eventually he sends her into retreat with a few other senior women students. Andrew addresses the women about their craving of affirmation from men. He says that they're not interested in truth as much as in being affirmed, and that they're using what they're good at, sex and service, to buy off the men so that they don't have to face themselves.

Andrew's focus on the women's conditioning becomes an increasingly central issue in the community. At the 1998 Rishikesh retreat, Andrew's pressure on the women reaches its peak. In a community meeting on the first day of the retreat, Andrew gives the women a taste of what is to come. He says that when he began to teach, it seemed to him that women have an easier time of it than men on the spiritual path. They are more in touch with their feelings, they're not too proud to show they're in ecstasy, they seem to surrender more easily, and they seem to love more deeply. But then he laughs his cackling laugh, as he usually does before he goes on to say something strong.

"But I've found over the years, that when they're challenged to allow real intimacy beyond feelings, beyond emotional devotion, women respond with a big NO!"

He shouts the last words and continues with a grim expression on his face, about how he felt a big "No" rising up in his meetings with the Sangha women. Suddenly he would feel a wall of fear and aggression without knowing where it came from. He says he didn't understand. Women seemed to have less ego; they were much more willing to serve others, much more generous.

"But I've found out that that's where their ego hides, that's where it takes refuge."

Andrew pauses. My thoughts drift off to an incident that happened last night. Clara, one of Andrew's long-time students, had complained about the heavy work schedule in the kitchen and the absence of free time. Andrew became furious when he heard about it. "I know her," he shouted, "she's always whining!" He ordered the other women to throw her bedding and her personal belongings out of the window. When Clara returned from her kitchen shift that night she'd found herself homeless.

The silence in the room deepens. Everybody feels uncomfortable, including the men. Andrew bends forward and says in an almost confidential tone, "For women it's a lot harder to come together, it's a lot harder to trust. Their ego is more insidious. They can be friends on a personal level and be very open with each other, but coming together in an impersonal way — they don't want to touch that with a ten-foot pole! They become competitive and mean to each other, and rip each other to pieces!"

Doubt raises its persistent head again. A few days ago Andrew ordered all the women students to take a cold bath in the Ganges, I think as a kind of repentance ritual. One of the women was suffering from a concussion, and she pointed out to the (female) Sangha doctor, that it may be dangerous to bathe in cold water with a concussion. Although, as a medical doctor she knew it wouldn't be without danger, everyone had to bathe. "Is this what impersonality means?" Doubt asks. "Nothing is personal therefore everything is allowed to get each other to change? No concern for individual feelings is necessary? Everyone is fair game since we're only shooting at the ego, not at each other?" I try to chase away Doubt. This is not being mean, it's showing compassion. Compassion can take many forms, not only the sentimental form we imagine. Things are black or white, and this talk about concussion danger was probably exaggerated.

Meanwhile, Andrew has dropped a bomb in the room with his last sentence, and at this point one of the men feels compelled to try to slow Andrew down.

"But aren't men much more competitive than women actually?"

Andrew nods. He says that yes, in the world, in their work, on a superficial level, men seem more competitive. But once they break through that, they can really meet. They can be really honest. Most women are never really honest with themselves and with each other. "It's too threatening," he says, "they feel it would literally be the end of them."

Andrew sighs, as if he feels confronted with an impossible mission.

"I've let it go for too long, but now I'm determined to take on the women's conditioning. I want all of you (he bends over toward the women) to crush this deep-seated biological programming and culturally determined ideas about what a woman is. I don't care what it takes. I mean it. It might mean that all of you run away and I end up with only men students."

Silence. Some of the men look at each other with worry in their eyes. The women sit with downcast eyes, crushed, not knowing what to say or do. Then Andrew breaks the silence. He says to the women, "I feel no response from you whatsoever. I don't know what to do anymore to reach you. Why don't you all leave now and have a meeting together. I want you to come up with a response."

One by one the women leave the room. When they're gone Andrew turns to us, his men students. In a confidential tone, he tells us how frustrated he feels with the women. They're just not getting it. He asks for our solidarity. We have to stand together as men in this historic fight against a deeply rooted archetypal conditioning. "No one has taken this on before," Andrew says. He tells us that the women are mainly looking for affirmation; they want to keep the feeling that they're fundamentally okay. He warns us not to be taken in by their wiles, and asks us to deny them the affirmation they crave so badly. He advises us to approach them in a strictly formal way, not so much as smile at them, not to give them the feeling that things are okay. We assure Andrew that we're at his side in this war against the women's conditioning.

In the course of the retreat Andrew's measures against the women escalate. He humiliates them publicly in community meetings, he rants and yells at them. He wants the women to come up with a response, make a gesture. He forbids the women to apologize, since this is their built-in response to make things okay again. When some women make the mistake of apologizing, they are banished from the retreat. They move into the yoga ashram next door.

During one of the Sangha meetings, Andrew performs a little play with some of the elder students. They sit in a circle and imitate what goes on in women's meetings, ridiculing them further. The women are driven to despair. Andrew proposes the men break up all the relationships in the community, so that the women are left to themselves. Some men have problems with that, especially a Dutch student who also has a child. We give him a hard time about being so bourgeois. In the end the relationships are not broken up.

"Why is Andrew so harsh with the women?" Doubt asks me. "Could it have something to do with his difficult relationship with his mother—his mother who deserted him and who just a few months ago published a very critical book about Andrew called *Mother of God*. She tells the story of how her son met Poonjaji and became a guru. She describes life in Andrew's community as a kind of horror story. Andrew was furious when it came out, and spent long meetings with his students in Foxhollow, deriding the book, reading passages from it to show how utterly ridiculous and unfounded they were. Is Andrew projecting his anger towards his mother onto his women students?"

7

EXIT

You're evil!

-Andrew Cohen

7.1. A Combination of Freud, Wilber and Einstein

As tough as Andrew is on the women during this retreat, he is as friendly and sweet with the men. We feel he needs our emotional support in these trying times, and we give it freely. We meet frequently with Andrew, sometimes formally but more often socially. There is a sense of camaraderie and solidarity. We're Andrew's army, storming the barricades of the women's conditioning together.

However, with Andrew you can never be sure of anything. Towards the end of the retreat Andrew calls a formal meeting with the men. He's not satisfied with his older students. They should have more of a leadership role, be serving more as an inspiration to younger students by keeping the standard and thereby pushing others in the group beyond their limitations. This isn't happening enough, Andrew says. The old-timers are satisfied with a place in the pack rather than giving themselves completely to pulling the group as a whole to a higher level. That's why there's stagnation. I know I'm one of the old-timers he's talking about. But I don't feel I'm a potential leader at all, more a survival artist than a motivator. I have difficulty enough keeping my own Doubt in check, let alone being able to inspire others to passionately join in Andrew's crusade against the ego.

The next morning at seven-thirty he calls an emergency meeting. This is usually not a good sign. Andrew has thought more about yesterday's theme and feels he has been too soft with the old-timers. It's unacceptable how they are cruising, escaping their responsibility as role models. Dan especially undergoes Andrew's wrath. Dan is a Canadian student who's been around since the time of Amherst. He has been through the familiar pattern of rising up to be a leader and then crashing twice. He is now chastised extensively by Andrew about his selfishness, his "unreality" and his play-it-safe conformity. Instead of disintegrating into a sorry heap of misery, Dan extensively apologizes for behaving like such a bastard and promises he will change. He gets an ultimatum. He will lead the Boston community, starting immediately. If he fails, he's out. Dan says he's ready for this challenge and thanks Andrew passionately for this unique chance.

Then Andrew starts speaking to me. I freeze. Andrew tells the rest of the group that they might think I'm a friendly nice guy who wouldn't harm a fly, but underneath this harmless exterior hides a megalomaniac who sees himself secretly as a combination of Freud, Wilber and Einstein. Laughter. Then he says that over the past ten years I've caused him more trouble than any other student. No one is more stubborn. "I have to say that he's also been able to undergo more pressure than anyone else. And to his credit, he never doubted me." This is a dubious compliment which is not even true. If he only knew ... Andrew continues to admonish me for my selfishness, my superiority, my hiding out in the group without wanting to be a leader. He says when I do anything for others it's only to score points for myself. As an intellectual I feel above such menial tasks as cleaning or shopping. He doesn't know what to do with me anymore, but this needs to change, or else. I listen passively to all of it, nod in agreement at times but don't say anything. Unlike Dan, I'm of the persuasion that if you're being shaven, the best thing is to sit tight and not move. Andrew doesn't seem to expect a real response either. A public humiliation is enough. "Now you're in for it," says Doubt, "the others can now score points by criticizing you."

Once again I feel frustrated that Andrew is not interested in dialog. Of course I'm hiding out, but isn't he interested in why? Does he have no idea of the doubts that are living in me, or doesn't he want to know? Those doubts would probably be for him an exact example of my megalomania, a sign that deep down I even dare to put myself above Andrew and be convinced that he's wrong.

On my way out I briefly speak with Harry, who's also been present at the meeting. He doesn't say much, just that I have to change in a big way now, emphasizing the word "big." I can't help but notice though that Harry is not looking too good himself.

Doubt says, "What is all this talk about changing in a big way? This whole idea, that if you wanted to, you could choose to change radically right now? And that if you don't change right away, it means you're aggressively resisting, that you don't actually want to change; that you're ambivalent about how free you want to be? Why are we at each other's throats for the slightest mistake? Why is all failure suspect, always your own fault, no matter what the extenuating objective circumstances? When things don't work out, when anyone fails at something, we assume he's made a wrong choice somewhere. A mistake is never just what it seems to be but a reflection of a deeper moral failing, an impure motive hidden somewhere that led you to this inappropriate choice. Who decides whether Andrew's choices are appropriate or inappropriate?"

7.2. Disillusion

In February 1998, we are all back from Rishikesh. Marcel is not doing well, not holding himself to the standard. He is having doubts about our life together, about whether he wants to be part of the community. The other men students, especially me, are expected to take a strong stand with him and make it clear that his behavior is unacceptable. After a strong meeting with him, we tell him that he can't return to his community house—he has to go to a hotel and think about whether he wants to be part of the community or not. For two days he stays in a hotel thinking about what he wants. His decision is made more difficult because he is in a relationship, and leaving the community would mean leaving the relationship. Eventually Andrew sends Marcel a message—he wants him to come to Foxhollow to do a retreat. In Foxhollow there's now a permanent retreat going on where about ten students are getting up at three-thirty to meditate for three hours, do mantra practice and a thousand prostrations. Six hours in total. Afterwards they start their day jobs. We are relieved that Marcel will be joining the retreat. Marcel is also relieved. He can still be in his relationship, and a retreat in Foxhollow is a lot better than the daily grind of community life in Amsterdam.

Shortly afterwards another male student from Amsterdam comes under fire for not living up to the standard. He is sent off to Foxhollow to do the retreat as well, leaving only three of us in the men's group in Amsterdam. Because of the crisis the women are in, the men are supposed to take charge of the center.

In March, Marianne goes for a ten-day visit to Foxhollow, just as I did last fall. But her visit is a lot less pleasant. She is severely taken to task in the women's meeting for not taking a strong stand with the women's conditioning. When she comes back from Foxhollow, she's a wreck. The men are still under strict orders not to engage the women in conversation, to not even smile at them, in order to not affirm them and give them the sense that everything is alright. Those of us in a relationship have been told not to have sex with our partners. That would affirm them too much. This has an alienating effect on Marianne. Slowly I see her despair grow. It's painful for me to see her suffer like that and have to maintain a stern exterior to her at all times. I feel sad and alone. Deep emotional doubt starts to come to the surface. Am I going to allow the same thing to happen to Marianne that happened with Sarah back in Amherst? What is the meaning and purpose of this, behind all the rhetoric? What happened to the love? I feel an overwhelming desire to have my own life back. But I've just seen with Marcel where speaking of doubt leads, so I stay mum.

The pressure builds for everybody including Harry. To our shock he has to go to England into retreat. Apparently he has blown it, we don't know how. Now both Harry and Sophia are gone, and our Amsterdam community is leaderless. Dorothy, a student from Australia who has been around since 1987 and who is leading the German community now, comes to Amsterdam a few days a week to keep an eye on things.

In the beginning of April I get a phone call from Dan, the new leader of the Boston community. He tells me that Andrew wonders where I am at with everything that was pointed out to me in Rishikesh. He says I've been avoiding writing to Andrew, which is not a good sign, and that Andrew doesn't have the impression that much has been changing. I feel intensely under the gun. I still have to give more. I feel that I am, but no one else seems to agree. I feel trapped in a no-win situation. Everyone is asking something from me that I can't give, because deep down I don't agree with what they're asking me to give up: my individuality. Again I'm fighting myself, trying hard to satisfy my interrogators. I know where this kind of situation is leading — do I want to let myself go through all that again?

All the students go on a weekend retreat in the English seaside town of Worthing. Although Andrew is not there in person, Dan is there to deliver his messages. Dan speaks about the obligation to live what we have realized, the screaming imperative to be an expression of sanity. In this obligation there is no time to think about ourselves, to bargain with options of throwing in the towel, to entertain or otherwise get involved with fear or doubt. The task is huge, and it must be done. The whole community gets an extra practice from Andrew: six hundred prostrations, to be performed every morning. During each prostration, we have to repeat to ourselves the following mantra that Andrew has made up: to know nothing, to have nothing, to be no one. This is the message he wants engraved in our brain.

A typical day in community life now looks as follows: Get up at six. Do 600 prostrations until eight. Breakfast, and then off to our daytime jobs. During lunch break at work: one hour of mantra practice (under the guise of taking a stroll in the park). Back from work at six. Go to the center at six-thirty. Dine together in the center with the other students. Meditate from seven-thirty to eight-thirty with students and lay people. From eight-thirty until midnight: either volunteer work in the center for the FACE organization or a men's meeting or a combination. Between eleven and twelve we often have a conference call with students in England, Germany, or Foxhollow. In bed around one.

The pressure in the Amsterdam community continues to escalate. In the women's meeting the women are learning to yell at each other and to kick each other out of a meeting when someone is not coming through. Also in the house things heat up. When Erica is going through a rough spot, her roommate is encouraged to take a stand — she refuses to sleep in the same room with her, and Erica has to sleep in the attic, a humiliating thing. But two weeks later the roles are reversed. Things are looking more and more like a madhouse. My doubts get stronger. Is this sanity? The pressure on both Marianne and me increases week by week. I'm not allowed to speak with Marianne about it. I am being called a selfish jerk, all my attempts to show good intentions are dismissed as insincere.

There is still no sign from Harry. I miss him. His situation reminds me of when John went into retreat. It is inconceivable to us that Harry won't make it, but it is looking possible. I try desperately to push my doubts away. I try my best to be a leader, to put the squeeze on others even more fanatically. I see myself become cold and harsh, inhuman, all in the name of the revolution. The pattern is so clear: to stay on Andrew's good side I'll have to violate myself and others more and more. What does this have to do with freedom? I go too far a few times, am too harsh against others, so now I become a target for that. Dorothy tells me that I'm acting like a dictator, like Hitler even. I'm no longer even surprised by that kind of rhetoric, or able to take it seriously.

Robert, my old nemesis from the book crisis, who now leads the London center, stops by for a visit in

Amsterdam. I am one of the problem cases to be addressed. Robert and I go through the familiar motions. He gives me a speech about how inexcusable, how truly outrageous my behavior is, how I'm saying "no" to Andrew, "no" to love, "no" to evolution. I apologize and promise I'll mend my ways and that I'll go for it. But my conviction is wearing thin. Marianne also has more and more doubts. We talk about how we can find an honorable way to step down. We are both still too attached to Andrew and his teaching to leave altogether. We just want to get ourselves out of the firing line, since we feel it literally drives us crazy. We speak about becoming lay students instead of formal students. I am interested in reading Luna's book about Andrew, and at the same time I'm afraid of what it will do to me. I tell Dorothy about wanting to read the book, and she suggests I ask Andrew if I may read it. I put in a message to Andrew with that request, and he answers in the affirmative. "Go ahead, but you need a strong stomach," he warns me. When I read Luna's book, it's just as I suspected deep down. Many of its stories and anecdotes match my own experience. Luna writes about our friendship in Amherst, the house meetings with Sarah and me, how I don't defend Sarah. It's painful to read but it's true.

7.3. The Last Week

It's a sunny Saturday afternoon. Marianne and I sit together on a terrace looking out over one of the busy Amsterdam streets. We talk it over together one last time. Tomorrow we're going to do it. We both feel that things can't continue like this. We're going to tell Dorothy that we don't want to be formal students anymore, but lay students.

Marianne is worried. "Andrew will be furious," she says, "he's going to send us away altogether."

I try to reassure her. "I don't think so. As long as we're honest, and stay with the truth at this moment, he will respect that." Doubt chuckles. "Do you actually believe that?"

Trying to convince Doubt, as well as Marianne, I continue, "How could something truthful not be in agreement with Andrew's teachings? There's no point faking a commitment we no longer feel. Andrew says that everybody around him will eventually find out how serious they really are. Enlightenment is just not the most important thing for us. He'll respect that."

Marianne is not convinced "Do you remember how he yelled at Erica, when she said she wanted to step down?" she asks. "And what about Marcel? Andrew was furious with him."

"It will be difficult, but we can handle it. We'll find a house together somewhere in Amsterdam, we'll still go to the meditations and video showings, and stay involved with the center as volunteers. It'll be okay." I take her hand into mine and squeeze it affectionately.

"Really?" asks Doubt.

From nine to one is Sunday meditation practice in the center. Afterwards I ask to speak with the other Dutch men. They walk with me up to a room on the first floor. There I drop the bomb. I don't want to be a formal student anymore. They look at me as if I've gone crazy. "That's impossible," they say. "No way." But I also see worry in their eyes. They hadn't expected this. They are unsure how to respond.

Meanwhile Marianne has a similar conversation with Dorothy. Then I am called in. Dorothy is furious. She speaks about treason, says we're sticking a knife in Andrew's back. "What am I supposed to tell Andrew?" she says. She sends Marianne and me away, into town. We should think about things separately and come back in a few hours.

I walk through the streets and feel an ecstatic sense of freedom. The future is inviting me. I walk past a bookshop window, from now on I can decide myself what I read and don't read. I sit down on a terrace and order a coke. Then my cell phone rings. It's Dorothy. She summons me back to the center to participate in a discussion group. There is no way I can disobey if I still want to be involved with Andrew in any capacity. So I head back to the center. The discussion group is focused on an excerpt from *My Master is My Self*, Andrew's first rapturous book about his meeting with Poonja. With six people in a circle, we discuss the excerpt. The sentences roll out of my mouth, about freedom, about the Absolute, about surrender. I can almost dream it by now. This is a completely insane situation. I feel as if I'm participating with the others in an absurd role playing game. For whose sake? For the sake of my soul probably. Dorothy most likely thinks the contact with Andrew's teachings in this discussion group will bring my soul back to life, will free me from the terror of my own mind, and bring back my inspiration. But doesn't she realize that it's exactly the other way around? It's my soul which is desperately gasping for air, it's only my mind that can still be tempted by Andrew's ideology.

After the discussion group Dorothy tells me there's a message from Andrew. It is completely unacceptable for him that I become a lay student, he says. He has put too much energy into me over the course of all these years. I have two options: fighting on as a formal student, or leaving altogether. This is the all-or-nothing situation that I've tried to avoid. Dorothy says I can think about it. "And what about Marianne?" I ask. Dorothy says that Andrew has sent her away. "Go back to your mama," he said. I am furious.

An hour later there is a telephone call from Foxhollow. Dan is on the phone. He asks me what my decision is. I am still not prepared to consider leaving Andrew, so my survival instinct kicks in. I tell him that I want to fight on. "Good" he says, "we all have to stand by Andrew in these difficult times." Marianne has also come to the center. She is in tears when she hears Andrew's message to her. I am ashamed of my betrayal. We should have become lay students together. Marianne doesn't think so however. She's glad that I'm continuing to fight.

We spend the night in separate community houses. People feel it's better if we don't spend time together so that I won't be weakened out of sentimental reasons. I hear the other students have spoken with Andrew on the phone. Apparently he has said that it's sometimes necessary to have blood on the streets, that that's part of his way of teaching. The blood is indeed on the street— Marianne's and mine. Why am I actually doing this?

On Monday morning I'm back at work. It's hard for me to concentrate. I call Marianne at her job. She's not going back to Germany, she will just continue at her job in Amsterdam. I'm happy about that. I tell her how furious I am about what Andrew is doing to her. She doesn't know what to say. She still encourages me to continue with Andrew. Is that more important for her than our relationship? Is it for me? I am furious with Andrew but it is unacceptable for me to leave him. I still feel there is a bond between us which I can only call sacred.

In the meantime I've been reading Luna's book. In the last chapter she describes the seven characteristics of dysfunctional families. I recognize them immediately in my experience of the community. To vent my anger, I write a letter to Andrew describing in detail how we, his students, are subject to those seven principles. I don't actually send the letter, which would be the same thing as leaving him, something I'm still desperately trying to avoid.

After work I buy flowers for the other students. White lilies. I write a sorry note with it. It's not heartfelt, but I know I can't do anything less. In the center we eat together and then meditate. Everyone tries to act as if nothing is the matter. Probably they're afraid to push me over the edge. Late in the evening there is a phone call from Foxhollow. A group of six men is on the phone. They have the same cautious approach, but dare to take some more risks. They push me to write to Andrew and to send him flowers. I know like no one else that that's the thing to do. They give me feedback about having been so weak. I tell them I am sorry about my moment of weakness that led me to want to be a lay student. "I don't know what came over me," I say. Of course I know very well what came over me, because it's still there. I feel torn between my loyalty to Andrew and his revolution, and the fury that is raging within me. One of the two has to die.

The next day I force myself to send an email to Andrew, with apologies for my behavior. I feel repelled, but it's something I have to do. I also have flowers sent to Foxhollow. That evening in the center Dorothy yells at me again. She is furious about the flowers from yesterday. White lilies are funeral flowers, and my apology to Andrew was too meager and not heartfelt. She has four women students meet with me. I understand that this is meant as an extra humiliation. When even the inferior women can give me feedback, it shows that my status is below zero at the moment. I don't care. I just let the harsh words come at me and I give the right answers. Where is this going?

On Thursday morning I wake up and know that I'm not going to work today. I call in sick. There is no one home, I am alone. I call a friend of mine and explain my situation to him. I ask if I can come over right now. I am very relieved when he says yes. I get dressed and take the train to his house. My friend is about sixty-years-old, a retired psychotherapist. I studied psychology with him, and I've stayed in contact with him over the years, even though he's been critical about Andrew.

I feel completely torn and confused. I want to leave Andrew, yet I feel bound to him by an absolute sense of loyalty. I don't believe in his revolution anymore and yet I feel guilty for doubting him. Like Faust I feel tormented by two souls, and paralyzed as a result of it. The fact that I'm looking up my friend now shows which soul I want to kill—the soul that hangs on to the relationship with Andrew, that can't let go of the ideal of enlightenment. I feel like an alchemist looking for ways to manipulate the various parts of my soul, to break the deadlock, so that the decision I want to take can be taken by the stronger part. I no longer feel an autonomous agent, capable of independent decisions. Opposing forces are at war within me, and may the strongest one win.

In the study, its walls lined with books, we sit on chairs opposite each other, each with a cup of tea. From what I tell my friend it becomes very obvious that I want to leave Andrew. Yet he tells me to take my time, don't rush any decision, and don't let things escalate to an irreparable conflict.

In the afternoon I go back to Amsterdam and sit on a terrace. I should finally write that letter to Andrew. That letter of goodbye. I struggle with writing down the simple statement that I am leaving without burning my bridges behind me. Whatever I try, I know it's insufficient. Is there a way to leave honorably? Dutifully I show up at the center for dinner and meditation. Everyone sees that I look like a ghost. They all avoid me. I think it's better like that. Someone asks me how I'm doing. My answers are not encouraging, I can tell from her face. She encourages me to hang in there, don't give up. From a sinner I've become a patient.

That evening, as I'm ready to go to bed, there's a phone call from Foxhollow; a message to call Andrew back. So finally it's time for the master himself to get involved. I pick up the phone and dial the number. There's Andrew's voice on the other end of the line. Now it will all be decided...

7.4. The Last Phone Call

Andrew digs in right away. He says he's heard bad things about me, that the people in Amsterdam don't know anymore what to do with me. He says that's unacceptable for him.

As usual, his intensity has an overpowering effect on me. I take a deep breath.

"Well, Andrew, last Sunday I asked to be allowed not to be a formal student anymore, and actually I still think that would be best. I don't have it in me to be a formal student right now. I've run out of gas. What I'd like to do is to step back for six months or so, to recharge my batteries."

Andrew laughs derisively. He says that's the stupidest thing he's ever heard. What good would that do?

There's no turning back now. I have to continue even though I know he will disagree.

"Andrew, the nine months of the hundred rebirthing sessions had a positive effect on me. They helped me to strengthen my clarity of intention."

I realize that the comparison is moot. I just want out, but I want out without burning my bridges behind me. I'm like a lawyer negotiating a deal, trying to find an exit strategy.

Andrew is not in the mood for bargaining. He's unwavering.

"Then you would leave for six months and come back as the great Andre who's done it again? Your ego would be restored, and you'd have the strength to last another few years. That doesn't have anything to do with my teaching. Tell me, Andre, does that have anything to do with my teaching?"

I sigh. "No, Andrew."

"What is my teaching? It doesn't matter what you think. It doesn't matter what you feel. It only matters what you do."

I think back to Jose's song. That seems so long ago; when the four of us undertook our desperate attempt to get back into the community. And now Jose has left, Donald has left, and I?

Andrew's voice goes up another notch, as he tells me that there are moments in life where we just have to respond blindly, blindly leap forward into the unknown without worrying about the consequences, without worrying about ourselves. He says my response has been pathetic since last Sunday, that I didn't even apologize properly to everyone about what I had done.

"Yes, Andrew."

"Listen Andre, I don't give a damn about your personal evolution anymore. I just want to be able to use you for my community. I need you in Amsterdam. Even that asshole Harry is letting me down now. Robert says he's not coming through. He's really a jerk."

I am shocked that Andrew speaks that way about Harry, who has been a hundred times more loyal than I've been over the years. Harry has given his life to Andrew. What more could Andrew possibly expect from anyone?

Apparently Harry's retreat is not going well. Probably, like John before, Harry is now being crushed to bits.

"Andre, you just have to do it now. If you don't do it now, your eleven years with me don't mean a thing. It will all have been a big lie!" I feel myself getting angry. If Andrew is trying to get a rise out of me, he's succeeding. But I won't give him the satisfaction of showing him.

Andrew continues ranting that everything he said about me in Rishikesh was an understatement, that I don't want to give anything, that I haven't understood his teachings at all. He says with all my cleverness I'm making a mockery out of his teachings. "You have no idea what real love is all about. I feel you're messing with me, Andre. You're not taking me seriously."

My heart is beating loudly in my chest. It physically hurts to hear him saying this. But at the same time I feel a strange detachment. I don't feel any contact with him whatsoever. Doubt asks me, "So this is the man you fell in love with eleven years ago? This is the man who loves you unconditionally?" I don't have the energy to answer Doubt anymore. Does this man love me? Or is he just furious with me because I'm an unreliable factor in his machine? Because he can't use me as he wants to? Does 'care for the whole' actually mean "care for Andrew's community?" Does 'Thy will be done' mean "Andrew's will be done?"

I listen to Andrew's voice, getting ever more high-pitched, with resignation. I'm running on empty. It's like when Andrew yelled at me in Rishikesh, only ten times worse. Doubt continues, "Is this your enlightened spiritual teacher on the phone, or an emotional five-year-old throwing a temper tantrum?" I don't know. At best it's both.

"All right, Andre. I want to hear your answer now. What's it going to be? Are you going to go for it?"

Silence. I feel utterly paralyzed. What can I say to Andrew? I'm sorry and that I'll do anything to better my life? Just like I said to Robert a few weeks ago? I can't get it past my lips. Get furious with him and tell him he's behaving like a little child? I'd like to do that but I still feel bound by a thin thread of loyalty, based on I don't know what.

The silence extends three seconds, five seconds. I can feel Andrew getting angrier every second.

"Andre," he explodes, "you're not responding. You're holding out on me. This is so aggressive what you're doing. You're totally in the grips of your megalomaniac ego."

"Yes, Andrew," I manage to bring out, still paralyzed.

"I can't tolerate this, Andre. You're jerking me around. No one has ever jerked me around like you have over the years."

I don't say anything. Then Andrew's voice barks at me again, enunciating the words clearly.

"Andre," he says menacingly, "you are evil!"

There's a click and the telephone connection is broken. I stand with the receiver in my hands. I notice sweat is poring down my face. My t-shirt is soaked. Did I hear him correctly? Did he actually call me "evil" just now? I slowly exhale, noticing that I have been holding my breath.

I know one thing very certainly now. The spell has been broken. These last three words have snapped the elastic of our relationship. I can't believe that someone who calls me evil has the best intentions for me. There are certain human boundaries that must be respected. I feel angry, sad, relieved, determined. So this is it. This is the end of eleven years of my life. The fairy tale is over.

8

ENLIGHTENMENT BLUES

It doesn't matter how much time you have spent with a Teacher – if Liberation wasn't given, then move on. Don't be attached to no-enlightenment.

-Andrew Cohen

The next morning I pack up all my belongings to leave. Fortunately everyone is out working, so there is no one to stop me or talk me out of my plans. I write a brief note to Andrew to tell him that I am leaving. I feel shattered, but at the same time I feel a huge relief.

I spend a quiet weekend with my parents, still reeling from the events of the past days. I can't quite grasp the enormity of what has happened. Have I just walked out on my guru? On an eleven-year commitment that I always thought would be for life? Marianne comes over to stay with me and we go for long walks, barely talking, both still too stunned to say much.

A few days later I get a message from Andrew, via Dorothy, who calls me at work. Andrew is outraged at my behavior but he wants to give me a last chance, she says. He wants me to come to Foxhollow and do a six-month retreat. I decline the offer. Some days later I am called by several of my old buddies from Foxhollow, who plead with me not to give up the battle. I am just temporarily in the throes of my ego, they say, and I shouldn't throw away my one chance in this lifetime for enlightenment. Why don't I give it one more chance?

Over the next few days I consider it. Why don't I give it another chance? What do I have to lose? Maybe an intensive retreat will get me to rise up beyond myself. Maybe I can realize deep and powerful insights in the silence there, far away from the distractions of worldly life. Remember how it was in the retreat in Katmandu? It brought me back to life after I was almost spiritually dead. Thinking about it like this, I almost want myself to want to do it. But a strong voice inside tells me it's the wrong thing to do. I know I don't want to go back. It's not good for me, it's damaging my soul. I feel that I would be sinning against myself by going back.

8.1. Marianne Goes Back

For the next five weeks, Marianne and I continue to live together in a narrow attic in my parents' house. Then we find an apartment in Amsterdam. We try to build a new life. Then, in June, Andrew comes to Amsterdam for his semi-annual public teachings. A few days after his arrival he invites Marianne to have a talk with him. He asks her to reconsider her decision to leave, says it was very extreme to run away from the community altogether. I am more than upset. Didn't Andrew send Marianne away himself? Didn't he tell her to go back to her mama?

Marianne however is touched that Andrew still loves her. She goes to the public teachings and is seriously considering going back to the community. She asks me to consider the same thing. But that is the furthest thing from my mind.

The fact that Marianne goes to Andrew's public teachings forces me to be clear about what I think and where I stand. One thing is clear: I no longer believe in the myth of Andrew's perfection. For so many years this was my unshakeable foundation. Andrew was not only enlightened, but also a pure and perfect human. That spell has been broken. Andrew is just a human like the rest of us, with his flaws and shortcomings. Nonetheless I still feel love for him and a sense of loyalty to his cause, of not wanting to obstruct it. I still think his teachings are valid. Whether or not his approach is working, if not for me then maybe for others, well, I'm willing to give that one the benefit of the doubt.

I still find it impossible to tell Andrew what I truly think. I'm afraid of losing him, even though I've lost him already. I want to be able to bow out gracefully, so I write Andrew a letter in which I praise his teachings in the same extravagant ways as before. Very carefully I state that, although I respect his mission, I don't want to be a part of it personally. I write that "in my previous many crises I never came to a point where I seriously entertained the option of not continuing, no matter how much struggle was involved, but now it is different. I still feel loyal to the truth of the teachings, to your integrity as a Teacher, and to the transformative potential of the community, but I feel that loyalty is not enough. I am not willing to engage in the ordeal of facing myself." The letter ends with the usual profound declarations of gratitude for everything that he has given me all those eleven years.

Doubt says, "Do you actually still believe in the 'transformative potential of the community' if you disagree with its approach in so many ways? Do you still 'feel loyal to Andrew's integrity as a teacher' if you feel he ranted at you like a five-year-old?"

But my feelings for him are complex. I don't fully understand them myself. I still feel gratitude for what Andrew revealed to me when I met him, that he put me in touch with my deepest inner nature, and allowed it to flourish. But as things go, Andrew turns out to make it easier for me to determine where I stand. With Andrew, there is no such thing as bowing out gracefully.

The next day I get a phone call from Dorothy. She tells me Andrew has received my letter, and asks if I still want to support the Amsterdam community? Specifically he asks me to donate 1500 guilders monthly to the community as a way to support Andrew's mission. Is this Andrew's answer to my letter? Is this the way I am supposed to show my respect for Andrew's mission? I tell Dorothy that I will consider it, but I already know that I don't want to give this money.

Later on that day Marianne comes home in tears. She had gone to see Andrew, to tell him she wants to come back into the community. Andrew told her that it is better for her not to be in a relationship with me then, because I will have a negative influence on her. He has said to her that my letter was understandable from a worldly point of view, but crazy from his perspective. I am furious. How does he have the nerve! To ask me for 1500 guilders a month, and simultaneously take away my girlfriend, the third one in a row! He's not getting a penny from me! I am now pissed that I wrote him such a generous letter. I kick myself for my naiveté. How many times do I have to be jerked around by this man until I stop being under his sway?

8.2. First Conversation with Harry

Harry has come over from London to Amsterdam to attend Andrew's teachings. He is still having a hard time. When he sees Marianne in the teachings he tells her it's a shame I'm not there. He would like to see me. I would like to see him too. He is the friend I miss the most. I call him up and we make an appointment.

"Thursday night I am moving," he says, "do you want to come and help me?"

"Moving?"

"Yes, I am emptying the house in the Rozenstraat. Some other students are going to live there."

He tries to say it with a light touch, but I feel a world of pain underneath. The house in the Rozenstraat was the house where Harry and Sophia lived for several years, until 1997 when Sophia had not met the expectations for a leader in Amsterdam. She was sent back to America to do intensive spiritual practice and their relationship was over. And now Harry himself is still in trouble and has to clear out of his house in the Rozenstraat.

On a Thursday night Harry and I carry boxes, mattresses, cupboards. It seems almost like old times. Once everything's in the moving van, we look for a café.

Harry tells me about his travails. Since March, when things started to go wrong, he's been under heavy pressure.

"I will spare you the details, Andre, but a side of my personality came up that was truly ugly, horrible." Since the fall of 1997, when Sophia had to go into retreat, Harry had been leading the Amsterdam center as well as the one in Cologne alone. Traveling back and forth between both cities, he tried to keep everything going. That had to go wrong sometime. I think back to a meeting with Dorothy, in April, when she blamed Harry for all the stagnation in the Amsterdam center.

Harry tells me more. He was sent to London to do a retreat. Robert came to talk with him every day, and yelled at him because nothing had changed. I think back at how Robert tortured me about Andrew's book. Yes, I know what it must have been like. Harry tells me how he looked into the mirror every day and wondered why he didn't leave. How he lived through the most horrible doubts about Andrew, the most intense fury.

"So what will happen now?" I ask

"Well," Harry says, "Andrew has been very generous with me. He's giving me another chance. He's told me to go to Australia for a year."

"Australia? But Andrew's center has just been closed there because there was too little interest! What will you do there, in the middle of nowhere?"

"I'll try to drum up some interest for Andrew's teachings. It's really a great opportunity!"

The more Harry tries to convince me how great this is, the sadder I feel. Harry is banished to Australia. Isn't that where they sent convicted prisoners?

"And what about you, Andre?" Harry asks.

I tell him my story; the phone call with Andrew, my refusal to do the retreat.

"So where do you stand now? Why don't you hang in there? I know it's been difficult for you, but I've had a very rough time too."

That's true. Harry has probably gone through ten times as much misery as me, but he has stayed loyal to Andrew. Harry had ten times as much reason to leave, but he continued to say "yes" where I said "no." In his own view he followed his heart where I, in all my weakness, started listening to my mind. Harry's still hanging on by the thin thread of loyalty that snapped for me. He still believes in the myth of Andrew. But what would happen to him if that illusion were crushed? Where would he go?

He grabs my hand.

"Did you forget, Andre? Sariputra and Mogallana? The two Buddhist friends that had promised to each other that they would stick together until they were enlightened?"

"Harry," I say softly but resolutely, "I don't believe in it anymore. It's not working. I know for sure that it would mess me up to stay with Andrew. There is no room for my individuality."

"That individuality of yours," Harry says bitterly, "that's just your ego. That's only the part of you that wants to say, 'look how great I am, look how intelligent I am, look how special I am'. That part of you is the enemy."

I notice there's no real conviction behind his words. Perhaps he's trying to convince himself as much as he's trying to convince me.

"I don't agree with you," I say.

What more is there to say then?

"Can't you just at least respect my choice?" I ask, against my better judgment. "Why can't you just say, 'I don't agree with the road you're taking, but I wish you well'?"

Harry looks at me with a wary expression on his face.

"Wish you well, Andre?" he says emphatically, "you're not doing well, and you won't be doing well."

I freeze. I hadn't expected he would go that far. It's almost a curse he's putting on me. Does he believe what he's saying? But if I take Harry's situation into consideration I can understand. He is just as much on the edge as I was a few months ago. Of course he's also plagued by doubt. And he probably knows that he's lost as soon as he gives an inch of room for the possibility that there may be something to those doubts, and that Andrew may be less than perfect. I understand his dilemma but I can't help him.

"Maybe we should go, Harry," I say, "we'll only be going around in circles."

Harry doesn't say anything and looks at the ground. Does he want to silence me to death? Is it unbearable to him how my soul is going to the dogs? Again I say, "Maybe we should go, Harry."

Very faintly he says, "Just go."

I sigh. Does a fifteen-year friendship have to end like this? It hurts.

"Well, I'll go then, Harry. Bye."

No answer.

Only when I'm walking outside on the Prinsengracht do I realize how sad, but also how angry I am. Harry and I now find ourselves on opposite ends of a wall, with no communication possible. It bothers me to see Harry like this. Why couldn't he just wish me well, even though we were no longer on the same track? What kind of community is this, where the people who leave are treated so negatively? Why is there so little room for disagreement?

8.3. Conversations with Marianne

With dinner just finished, Marianne and I sit at the kitchen table, each with a cup of coffee. Marianne looks sad. In two days I'll move out of our apartment. I've decided to rent a furnished room so Marianne can live by herself and make her way back into the community. She pleads with me once more to go back with her, but I tell her I will never go back.

"If going back to Andrew is what you want to do, then you should do it," I say.

"But can we still be friends then?" She asks.

"Yes of course," I say, "if Andrew will allow you to have a friend like me."

"Don't talk like that about Andrew," she says. And for the umpteenth time over the past week we get into a discussion about Andrew.

"Don't you remember what Andrew always said?" Marianne says. "The personality is like a mirror that is usually covered with dust. With enlightenment, the dust is burned away by the light of true insight and understanding, so that the mirror can be an untainted reflection of the absolute. So of course Andrew is perfect as a result of his realization."

I say I don't buy it.

"To me, in the first few years, Andrew could still laugh about his own personal failings and shortcomings, his fear of going through English customs, or his neurotic worrying about vitamins. But then he started to believe in the myth of his own perfection, and lost control over his own unconscious needs for power and domination. He felt that the powerful enlightenment blast with Poonjaji had wiped out his ego completely, and that he had no shadow anymore. But being worshipped all day by hundreds of followers is bound to stir up any traces of narcissism still left in the personality. I think Andrew couldn't carry the weight of everything that we were projecting onto him, that he caved in under the weight of his own narcissism. And when he started criticizing Poonja, Trungpa, Da Free John, Rajneesh, Muktananda and all these other gurus for not being perfect, that only increased the pressure to be perfect himself. The more Andrew exposed the shadow in all these other gurus and their communities, the more he had to prove that there was no shadow in himself and his own community."

"And I think he did prove that and is still proving it!" Marianne says with conviction, "I don't see where

Andrew's behavior is not perfect. Where is this so-called shadow of Andrew? I only see a beautiful human being."

For me some other memories come to the surface; Andrew as the cold, distant, authority figure. Andrew enjoying the company of those students who tell him what he wants to hear. Andrew flying into a rage and shouting that so and so is a jerk, and so and so is a loser. Andrew calling me "evil" over the phone.

"Well, I feel it shows especially when it comes to control and power. You know how Andrew had total control over all of our lives. Look at what he did to me when I was working on his book. Or when Gina and I were in a relationship and he broke it up."

"So what's so bad about control?" Marianne says. "In some situations you need control. A football coach has absolute control over his players."

"Yes, but not over their private lives."

"Okay, but still. An abbot has absolute control over the monks in his monastery."

"Yes, that's because the monks don't have private lives, their lives are given over to God, or enlightenment."

"Okay, then maybe we lived like monks. What's so bad about that?"

"Well, in the case of monks, the use of power and control is acknowledged, and institutionalized. It occurs within a certain tradition. There are rules. All these things protect the monks so that there won't be misuse of power."

"Misuse of power, those are such big words! What are you talking about then?"

Yes, I think, what am I talking about? How can I accuse Andrew of misuse of power? And yet I feel compelled to follow this train of thought.

"Well," I start hesitantly, "the things Andrew had us do, and the suffering he put us through, were pretty extreme. He had absolute power. He knew that we were desperate to get his approval. Remember when Graham had to crush his 20,000 dollar car? Remember when Matt prostrated all the way up the hill to Andrew's house? The hundred rebirthing sessions?"

"Yes, but that was all to purify us! Andrew was simply pulling out the best in us. Of course we were all surrendering to him, that's what's supposed to happen between a spiritual teacher and a student. How else can the ego be overcome? Of course he was accepting and affirming our surrender to him. That's the job of a spiritual teacher."

"Well, of course he would say he's only trying to show us the light! It's nothing personal, the holy cause demands it, right? Just like the jihads, the crusades, the inquisitions! It's all to serve a larger purpose!"

I notice that I'm actually shouting. I tone down my voice a bit.

"You know, Marianne, Andrew always says there are no scandals around sex or money in his community. Everything is above board. But the problems weren't about sex or money, but about power. The power structures were never put in question, or hardly even spoken about. It was all considered self-evident and self-justified that Andrew himself was the absolute authority on everything. Power was the big taboo word, not money or sex. You remember how many letters we wrote. 'Beloved Master, you are the sun of my universe, you are the Buddha of our time; you are the unspeakable embodiment of perfection! O Master, I am not worthy of the privilege of being your student, but please forgive me all my devious sins'!"

I suddenly burst out laughing; the utter ridiculousness of it all leaps to my mind starkly. But Marianne is not amused. I continue, "All these ecstatic love letters that we wrote him, and that he loved us for. Remember that Andrew even published our love letters to him in a book? Is that narcissism or what? And why do you think that people convinced Andrew after a few years to take the book out of distribution? Everyone in the publishing world just took that book as a sign that Andrew was on a big ego trip!"

I can feel myself getting on a roll now.

"Look at what happens when people do not affirm him, admire him, look up to him. He flew into a rage when he felt that people didn't respect him enough. Remember how he would publicly denounce students who left, would say that they'd be haunted forever, would encourage us to shun them? Remember how he would let all of us write angry letters to the defectors who had hurt their Master so much by betraying him?"

Marianne furiously disagrees with me.

"Andrew is not narcissistic," she says. "Of course he is very hurt when people leave him, but that's because he's idealistic, that's something very different."

"Yes, idealistic," I say, "but idealistic in the way adolescents are idealistic. Remember how adolescents are?

You have these very noble but unrealistic ideals. Everything seems possible but you have no eye for the practical difficulties in realizing those ideals. You demand that everything changes 'right now' and 'totally', you view the whole world in absolute terms, things and people are good or bad, and qualifying something means compromising. Doesn't that sound a lot like how Andrew views the world? 'It's black or white', he always says. And he complains that none of the other teachers are as radical as he is. They all compromise. The thing is, most people have these youthful fantasies and look back at them later sadder but wiser, bemused by their early megalomania, thinking they would conquer the world with radical ideals. But in Andrew's case he actually managed to realize all his youthful fantasies, make them into a permanent lifestyle. And he managed to convince all of us to live in this way too."

I pause to let this sink in further. "After Andrew had become a spiritual teacher he had no need to go get over his adolescence because everything was still being done for him. He had never held a daytime job, he never had to earn a living. In his meeting with Poonja he was affirmed absolutely. The grandiosity of their mutual infatuation, Poonja's prediction that Andrew would start a revolution among the young in the West, all this didn't exactly help. So this is what Andrew brought to his work as a spiritual teacher. It manifested in his insistence that literally anything was possible; there were no limitations. This is the adolescent outlook on life, very attractive especially to other adolescents at heart, but in the end it was unproductive. The realities of life were consistently avoided, even denigrated. Andrew saw jobs and careers as a necessary evil, children and families as a mistake. He continually made parents feel guilty for having made the blunder of putting children into this world, and the children were subjected to the same regime as the grown ups. They even had meetings together where they told each other to take a stand."

Marianne is not convinced.

"You're just indulging in your anger and your cynicism," she says bitterly. "Why do you have to damage all the love? Can't you just humbly accept that it was too much for you without needing to throw dirt on Andrew?"

It's getting very late, so we decide to leave it at that for now. But as I'm lying in bed I can't help thinking about it more. Why did we all give Andrew so much power? Well, it was part of the whole system of course. You surrender unconditionally to your guru. That's a system that may have worked in the East, but does it work for Westerners? Can we just give away our individuality? Should we? More and more it makes me angry to think about how much I allowed myself to be abused. Why? Because I wanted to be enlightened so badly, and because Andrew was so convincing. But as the saying goes, power corrupts and all the power he had over us went to his head; especially once he put himself above his own guru. From that point on there was no one left who could put any limits on him.

A few days later I settle into my furnished room and Marianne starts going to the community meetings again. Even though she has decided to come back, she is still a bit of an outcast, on the lowest rung of the social ladder. When the whole community goes to the annual summer retreat in Switzerland, Marianne stays back in Amsterdam. She receives a lot of emails though about Andrew's teachings there, which she enthusiastically forwards to me. But now it all sounds stale. I find it hard to believe that only a few months ago I was willing to give up my life for these teachings. Is it just a matter of sour grapes? Am I trying to justify my decision of leaving? Or am I more objective now that I have some distance?

Meanwhile Marianne is not finding her way easily back into the community. She has to prove she's worthy to all the other students who don't fully trust her because she left. As a result she is lonely, and we continue to see each other. One evening we step into a restaurant when Marianne suddenly pulls me back. "Not here," she whispers, "let's go somewhere else."

"Fine, I know another place we can go to, but why?"

"I saw some people from the Amsterdam community sitting in there."

Marianne doesn't want to be spotted with me by the community members. They probably don't know she still has contact with me. I tell her this is the kind of thing that bothers me. I wouldn't want to be part of a community anymore that makes me feel paranoid about who I am spending time with.

Marianne doesn't agree. She reminds me of how close we were as a community, and how empowering it was for all of us to be together.

"Look how Andrew could always draw the best out of us and make us perform so well, you know, organizing public events, traveling trips, editing and publishing books, running centers."

"Yes that is true. For many of us, who might have been quite ordinary in the normal world, being part of Andrew's community was our chance to be part of a growing revolutionary movement, destined to overthrow the spiritual culture in the West. And we would share in that glorious fate. That was one of the carrots. Unfortunately, it never actually happened. And none of us really grew up; we didn't deal with our past, and we cut ourselves off from our parents, families, and friends. We stayed adolescents. The students emulate the teacher. Remember how we could never support ourselves financially, how everybody was just house cleaning and window washing to get by, year after year? How we were always thinking in absolutes? Who has actually changed after all these years? Nobody changed enough to be allowed by Andrew to live independently of himself and the community, let alone to teach others. So where are his results? How good a spiritual teacher is he?"

"It's our own fault that we're not changing. None of Andrew's students is really worthy of him. Our clarity of intention is not strong enough."

"Yes, but isn't it the job of any good teacher to get the maximum out of the student? Andrew just doesn't know how to deal with human imperfection. It doesn't fit into his ideas of perfection. He always overreacts, blows up at small mistakes that everybody else considers not such a big thing. He blows things out of proportion, creates a big drama."

"That's because he has much higher standards than we do. He wants to destroy any and all traces of ego that may not be so noticeable at first sight."

"Well, the result was that everything in the community was always centered on Andrew. Every time you had to make a decision you'd be afraid of making the wrong one, so you ran it by someone else who would run it by Andrew. And we would imitate the way he looked, dressed, moved about. We would watch the movies he watched, go to the concerts he went to, tried to second-guess his opinions on issues. We would then try to impress Andrew or others closer to Andrew, by denouncing each other, giving each other feedback. We could score points by making each other look bad. That was the way to demonstrate how loyal we were."

"That sounds ridiculous! So you think we were all victims of some totalitarian regime?"

"Well, I think we learned to accommodate ourselves to what Andrew's unacknowledged wishes and needs were. The ones who were best at reading and anticipating them became leaders in the community. They were good at serving Andrew, they were 'in the flow'. If Andrew was in a good mood, they could feed him uplifting news, flatter him, and project unrealistic expectations about the prospects of the revolution. If Andrew was in a feisty mood, ready for confrontation, they could feed him stories of students who were misbehaving, or some other issue that had to be addressed. If Andrew just wanted to hang out, they could hang out with him. The others of us who were less skilled at this kind of adaptation would suffer under Andrew's sudden wrath, his quickly changing moods, and his unpredictable outbursts."

"But in the community we learned how to trust in life and how to trust our own experience very deeply. We learned from each other how to go beyond our mind in order to let go into a deeper dimension of life. That's what we lived together in our profound intimacy!"

"I'm not sure anymore what it was that we shared together. Looking back, I feel that Andrew taught us to live in a state, in a particular hyperactive frame of mind that was called different things at various times. In the beginning it was called enlightenment, or being 'in the unknown'. Later on it was called 'keeping the impersonal perspective'. Being in such a state empowers you, energizes you. In a sense you are quite insulated from negative emotions, from the possibility of failure. Everything is possible, the sky's the limit. Like the hippies in *Hair*, we were getting high on each other all the time. Actually it was one huge bubble. As time went on, we had to do more and more mantra practice, meditation practice, prostration practice, to stay in that state. We needed to forcefully convince ourselves that this was it, that we were still spearheading human evolution on the planet. In that sense, the practice was effective, it kept the 'high' going."

"But what about learning to trust then? Didn't we learn to trust?"

"Actually I feel that my years in the community have made it harder for me to trust and surrender, because my trust in Andrew and the community has been betrayed so often. I never learned to trust my own intuition. I could only trust my own experience insofar as it didn't go against the grain of the community."

"But at least you learned how to never fit in and conform to the world."

"Well, yes, we learned to not fit into 'the world', but didn't we just replace 'the world' with "Andrew's world?" Wasn't it a rather closed and claustrophobic universe that we shared?"

"But we did learn to live together and speak about ourselves. We learned how to be emotionally vulnerable and speak honestly and openly about what we were feeling."

"Yes, but Marianne, how open was it really? Could we ever speak without having to be afraid what the others would say, or what Andrew would say? I feel it became second nature for me to lie about what I was thinking and feeling, to myself and to others, when it didn't fit with Andrew's teachings. We all learned to suppress our doubts. I do feel that I learned to think clearly and objectively in the discussion groups and the men's meetings. But it always stayed within the limits of Andrew's teaching, no matter how much we all talked about investigating everything and there being no taboos."

"Yes, but the meetings and all the talks did make us strong. We learned how to be courageous and persistent, how to face challenges. We learned how to survive under very difficult circumstances, disregard our doubts and never to give up."

"That's right!" I laugh. I know I'm provoking Marianne but I am angry. "We became spiritual warriors, well trained for the battle for enlightenment—the Jesuits of our time!"

That evening we have indeed been spotted in the restaurant. Marianne is taken to task for still associating with me. She has to make up her mind: the community or me. In tears, she comes to me and we talk for a long time. She says she wants to leave the community and get back together with me. I am not sure what to think about all this. I still feel hurt about what has happened, and I have the feeling Marianne wants to get back to our "partnership in the dharma" that we had when we both still believed in Andrew's revolution. I see a wide gap between us now. Marianne still believes in Andrew's revolution but feels too alone and insecure to fight on. I don't believe in it anymore. How can we be in a relationship? I tell her that we can be friends, and wait for a few weeks to see how it goes. She is desperate and wants to spend the night with me. I feel embarrassed and sad, and try to calm her down. Eventually she goes home alone.

* * *

Marianne decides to visit her parents in Germany and I go on a vacation by myself for two weeks. On the beaches of the Dominican Republic, I go for long walks and think about everything. Was it all just a pipe dream, an empty bag of broken promises?

On an emotional level I find my split with Andrew still very difficult. I realize how my main experience for the past six months since has been one of pain and loss. I still miss Andrew. But I can no longer believe in a perfection that is removed from human decency, from warm and loving personal attention, from kindness and encouragement, from vulnerability and self-deprecating ordinariness. The myth of perfection is too much like the myth of Narcissus. It is cold and heartless.

I know I will never go back. I want a life for myself, the freedom to make my own decisions, my own mistakes. I don't care whether my life is "evolutionary", but I want it to be authentic, my own life.

I return to Amsterdam with my head more clear. The day after I've come back, I call Marianne. She has had a very different vacation. She tells me excitedly that she has decided to return to the community. In Germany she has taken a long hard look at her life, and has come to the conclusion that her love for Andrew is the most important thing for her. She's over the moon about it. I guess now she will not be allowed to see me. Well, what can I say? Maybe it's better this way.

In December 1998, Andrew is in Amsterdam again for his semi-annual visit. This time I go to the teachings, to check out how it strikes me now. I am surprised that I don't feel any connection with him, that his teaching sounds like a broken record. His talk about killing the ego in order to find freedom now sounds fundamentalist to me. What was so thrilling about that? During his talk Andrew gives an example of the viciousness of the ego by talking about another student of his that left him a few days before, a rich American woman. He calls her a narcissist and speaks about how she once gave him two million dollars for his Foxhollow center, but was unwilling to give up her ego. I am shocked and upset by his derisive and aggressive tone of voice. He's throwing a tantrum in public at a student who gave him two million dollars! I find the whole thing unbecoming, to say the least. As a matter of fact I know the woman in question, and a few days later I manage to speak with her on the phone. She is devastated and outraged by Andrew's public treatment of her, not only because of the humiliation, but in particular because she had believed and trusted that Andrew would keep the two million dollar donation confidential. Listening to her story, a chilling picture emerges. Andrew had actually solicited the two million dollars from her, which amounted to over 80% of her total assets. She had been deeply upset and confused about what to do because she felt she could no longer continue to be his student if she said no. She loved the community, Andrew, and the spiritual path. Two of Andrew's students had talked to her repeatedly over several weeks. Finally she had given in and promised to donate the money. She believed it would be serving the world, since the estate of Foxhollow would allow others to have access to Andrew's teachings. Complicating matters, the money was not immediately available from a family trust. Andrew exerted pressure on her to rush the donation as he had already proceeded with the purchase of the property. The rushed transaction resulted in a loss of a great deal of money and she seriously risked losing her family relationships. In retrospect she described his request as a corruption of power. It's a story that makes me nauseous.

8.4. Ute

As I expected, I don't see Marianne anymore after she rejoins the community. It is a lonely time for me. Gradually I start to make more contact with other students who have left Andrew. One of them is Ute, a blond thirty-eight-year old yoga teacher who had also been involved with Andrew for eleven years. She's originally from Austria, moved to Amsterdam in her early twenties, traveled in India for a year, and met Andrew in that very same living room in Amsterdam as I did. She then moved to Amherst, Boston and California with Andrew's community, and was sent to Europe in 1995 to help out the fledgling German community in Cologne.

We know each other well from our time together in California where we lived in the same community house. Unlike me, Ute was never in a sexual relationship in the community, but was one of the people whom Andrew wanted to be celibate, which she was for seven years. She eventually left the community, early this year, because she wanted to be 'in the world' and be in a relationship. She still lives in Cologne.

We have long talks on the phone. I tell her about my experiences with Marianne, and she tells me about her attempts to build a new life for herself, trying to find a good job and a good man. We complain to each other about how difficult it is to get into a relationship with someone who doesn't understand what we went through with Andrew. I visit Ute for a weekend in Cologne. The visit turns out to be very nice, and she visits me back in Amsterdam. I realize that I'm falling in love with her.

Because I've mainly known Ute as a head shaven celibate, I never considered her someone I could fall in love with. Now I can't help but notice how beautiful she is. But more, with Ute I find the kind of emotional support and intimacy that I missed with Marianne. I feel loved for who I am, not for being a student who is living the teachings. Our relationship is not an impersonal one for the sake of the whole, but a very personal choice, for our own sake.

After a few months of traveling back and forth to see each other and extended daily phone conversations, we decide to live together. Ute moves to Amsterdam and we find a nice apartment together. We continue our investigation into why Andrew's revolution didn't work. Ute says there's a certain tragedy about it. So much would have been possible. In many ways Andrew was on to something, she says. He wanted to create an enlightened society, where people were less selfish and competitive; where they were giving and going beyond cultural and personal differences. I agree with her. But nobody could live the teachings in the way that Andrew wanted. Why not? That's the big question that Ute and I have many conversations about.

We try on Andrew's perspective on things. Maybe he did what he could. After teaching a few years he recognized that 'spontaneous enlightenment here and now' was too naïve, that people were not transformed just by an immersion in bliss. He then decided to create a formal community, a laboratory for living, with house meetings, men's and women's meetings. But after a while Andrew realized it was still not enough. No lasting change was produced, no transformation. Then he came up with spiritual practices in order to purify the soul, just like established religion has always done. And when that didn't produce the transformation that he was looking for, he came up with the idea of retreats, and periods of intensive spiritual practices. Again, just like traditional religion came up with the idea of monkhood and monasteries. From Andrew's perspective his revolution hasn't failed yet, it's just turned out more difficult than expected because human beings are so stubborn, so selfish, and have such tenacious egos.

But from another perspective Andrew's revolution was inherently flawed from the start because of Andrew's own personal shortcomings (especially his conviction that he had none). And because of the inherent limitations that arise when you import an authoritarian Eastern system of a guru, with disciples, to the West, with our respect for individual autonomy and creativity. Andrew didn't account for individual differences. His teaching was of the "one size fits all" variety. There was never any room for personal initiative, or personal experimentation with life.

Ute and I come across the book by Joel Kramer and Diane Alstad, *The Guru Papers*. It is an eye-opener for both of us. It shows us the seductions, predictable patterns and corruption contained in the relationship between gurus and disciples. Kramer and Alstad point to the simplistic mechanisms that are at work in this kind of relationship (it's all about control and surrender), and to the very sophisticated justifications that exist (the very powerful idea of enlightenment, absolute liberation). They say that it's not even necessarily that the gurus themselves are corrupted personally (although they can be), but that the abuse of power that happens is structural, not personal. The authoritarian situation where a charismatic guru has absolute power over his followers is in and of itself bound to generate unhealthy mechanisms. The disciples project perfection onto the guru. When the guru accepts the projection, he's in trouble.

This helps Ute and me to see our struggle with Andrew in less personal terms, and to be less angry and outraged with him. We joke that finally we are learning to view our time with Andrew from an impersonal perspective. There was nothing special about our time with Andrew. We've been members in just another cultish group that makes its members feel special. Our experiences are fundamentally no different from countless others in spiritual and political groups. We see clearly that corruption is difficult to avoid when a charismatic individual is given absolute power over a group of followers. All authoritarian groups have more or less the same dynamic. The emphasis on surrender, the initial happiness of merging into something bigger, the dogmatism, the rules and regulations, the suppression of doubts, it's the same thing everywhere.

Kramer and Alstad write about the two phases of spiritual communities, the messianic and the apocalyptic. In the messianic phase everyone is convinced that the world will soon embrace their revolution. The atmosphere is party-like. When the realization dawns that no such thing will happen, that the world disagrees with their revolutionary message, or even worse, doesn't seem all that interested in it, the atmosphere switches. Now the world becomes the enemy, the group becomes more isolated. In this apocalyptic phase the teacher responds by placing even higher demands on the disciples, demanding conformity, obedience, loyalty and devotion from them. A shrinking group of disciples has to work harder and harder to keep everything going. The teacher has monuments erected to himself.

To me and Ute this seems to be the phase that Andrew and his community entered into a while ago. The purchase and renovation of the Foxhollow estate seems like such a monument. It is too grand, a few sizes too big for the actual needs of the community, and the students have to bleed for it, with time, money and effort.

Andrew continues to speak publicly about his frustration with his students who are not serious enough. Luna's book generates some critical articles about Andrew and his community in *Quest Magazine*, the *Boston Globe* and the *LA Times*. Andrew responds with a little book called *In Defense of the Guru Principle*. Reading this seems to confirm our worst fears about where Andrew is headed. He maintains that the whole spiritual establishment is out to see him fail, because the vested authorities are afraid of his revolutionary ethical stance. No one understands his radical message, everyone is against him, and no one will believe that he has no shadow.

8.5. Second Conversation with Harry

On April 30, 1999, Ute and I go into the Vondelpark together to celebrate Queens Day, a Dutch holiday. Everywhere in the park children's activities have been organized. Andrew's Amsterdam community is represented with a theater for children, dartboards, second-hand clothes, and food. It is an important fund raising event for the community. On a sudden whim, I decide to stop by the stand. I shake a few hands and formal, distant polite remarks are being exchanged. Marianne is there but I have the impression that she pretends not to see me. Then I suddenly see Harry, wearing a big cowboy hat. In spite of our disastrous last meeting I am happy to see him. I walk towards him and shake his hand. He is happy to see me too. He tells me he has returned from Australia just last night after his year of exile. He's going to lead the center in London because Robert, who's always been in charge there, is having a hard time. I manage to suppress a smile. At least the suffering in Andrew's community is divided evenly and democratically. (I hear that at a later Rishikesh retreat, Robert was told to shave his head, had to wash all the dishes during the entire retreat, and then was sent to Australia.)

Harry and I go for a walk in the Vondelpark. He asks me how I'm doing now, and whether I'm considering coming back. I tell him that I'm not coming back, that I don't regret my decision.

"But," Harry calls out with his hands spread out widely, "now you're nothing more than all these people here in the park, ignorant and lost in their ego, people that only live for themselves!"

Although this perspective has also been mine for so long, its arrogance stops me in my tracks. Does everyone in Andrew's community feel themselves so elevated above the rest of mankind? I say to Harry that when I look back on it, I find my time with Andrew not so elevated above the rest of mankind.

Harry says he's never heard anything so stupid.

"How can you say that?" He asks incredulously. "We were giving our lives to something as radical and absolute as enlightenment. Have you forgotten all about enlightenment, Andre?"

"All that talk about enlightenment sounds very noble," I say, "but what is the actual result? Enlightenment implies that you can cure yourself from the disease of the ego once and for all. I don't believe that anymore. I believe more in ongoing care and attention, without an end point where all your conflicts are fully resolved. Maybe our conflicts are never fully resolved; maybe our character will never change radically. We talked about radical change for eleven years but nothing ever changed!"

"We've all realized that enlightenment is not as easy as it seemed at first. But Andre, when you were with Andrew, at least you were trying to transcend your ego! Now you're just wallowing in it, and that's apparently all right with you. What you tried to keep in check then, you're giving free rein now."

"Harry, I think that anything you try to kill will only return more strongly in a hidden way. I believe much more in outgrowing the ego in a natural way, like children get over their childish attachments and preoccupations when they grow up. I believe more in an integration of the personality, not in some kind of purification that would lead to rising above it and being liberated from it."

"Don't you realize that this personality you're trying to integrate is illusory! This sense of 'you' being special, that's just an illusion. It's all impersonal!"

"That sounds very good, but look at where it led to. I think we all became brainwashed. There was no room anymore for any display of strong individuality, any deviation from the norm, any self-interest apart from the group interest, any private life apart from community life."

"That's spiritual evolution, that's what it means to live only for the sake of the whole!"

"I don't buy it. This approach to spirituality may create loyal foot soldiers, but I feel it prevents us from growing up into healthy, morally autonomous, responsible human beings."

"Nonsense! Andrew wants us to become moral and responsible human beings. That's why he speaks about volition and taking responsibility for all of our actions, about doing the right thing."

"Yes, but the right thing was always what Andrew wanted us to do. Can you give one example of someone who made his own choice and stood by it, even when Andrew disagreed with it?"

"Andrew sees more clearly than us, how can we put ourselves above him? He's our master!"

"So the best you can become is a good Andrew-citizen. That's not my idea of true spirituality."

"I'm shocked, Andre, that you can say things like that and appear to be so happy with yourself. Don't you realize what a horrible choice for the ego you're making?"

And so once again, we stand opposite each other. Just like last year, no real contact seems possible.

9

EPILOGUE

At long last the horizon appears free to us again, even if it should not be bright; at long last our ship may venture out again, venture out to face any danger; all the daring of the lover of knowledge is permitted again; the sea, our sea, lies open again: perhaps there has never been such an "open sea".

— Nietzsche

9.1. Life After Andrew

It's been five years since I've left Andrew. Ute and I have built a new life for ourselves in Amsterdam and are very happy together. It's a wonderful experience to be in a relationship which is based simply on the pure joy of meeting each other and being together. I'm teaching philosophy at high school and at university now, and I'm about to complete a philosophy Ph.D. thesis on Nietzsche. I give lectures in and around Amsterdam on Nietzsche and Zen, and on modern spirituality. Ute is working as a yoga teacher and a high school German teacher. It's taken us years to get reoriented to a "normal" life within society, a life seemingly no longer focused on the constant pursuit of "radical and utter transformation." But actually the lives that we lead now feel a lot less closed off and dogmatic than our lives with Andrew. To us, this way of living seems more spiritually alive.

One of the more exhilarating experiences for me has been one of intellectual liberation. The quest to understand has taken on a new life, free now from the proscribed answers of the ideology that had once silenced my critical thinking. It's thrilling to experiment with life, be passionately engaged with it, and to find my own answers. I find myself more willing to think creatively, look at life from different angles, and to tolerate different perspectives. What does it mean to live as an ethical person? What does it mean to find meaning and purpose? Does something like unselfishness really exist? Or are selfishness and selflessness always intertwined and embedded, like two sides of the same coin? If a person was enlightened, what would that look like? And what's wrong with being me, instead of being transformed or enlightened?

Gina, Sarah, John and Robert are still with Andrew. Harry left in 2000 and has lived in Costa Rica since then. For the past six months he has been travelling, and he has stayed with Ute and me several times. I feel happy to have him back as a friend.

I haven't seen Marianne for the past five years, except once when she unexpectedly approached me in November, 2001 to go out for a coffee with her. Andrew had been teaching the night before in Amsterdam. Over coffee, Marianne told me that things were very different in the community now. Students were not so harsh on each other anymore and the focus was on the mutual love and intimacy. But my own impression, based on my contact with former students since I have left the community, is quite the opposite. The atmosphere in the community seems to have become grimmer, and an "us and them" mentality seems to be growing (we the chosen few, versus them, the ignorant world at large). Andrew's punitive measures against students that break the rules seem to continue. Many students leave, some of them even sneak out in the middle of the night. As one of them told me, he packed his bags, climbed out of the window, and called a taxi from his mobile phone.

Andrew is still teaching internationally. His journal *What is Enlightenment?* has become a glossy, four-color magazine, and is for sale in bookstores everywhere. His multinational communities are still functioning, although many of the original students have left.

* * *

After I left Andrew's community, I started looking for answers as to why I joined him, and why I stayed so long. I sought to explain my behavior by delving into my own psychology. Already, as a young boy, I had sought truth in God, and romantic redemption in Carla. These merger fantasies neatly coincided with Andrew's meeting with Poonja—such a disarmingly sweet young American who had merged with the absolute and invited me to surrender to him, in order to be united with God as well.

Seen from a certain perspective, my time with Andrew was a botched love affair. In Amsterdam, I fell in love with

Andrew, life was suddenly great, love was unconditional (you and I are one in the absolute). In Amherst Andrew's love started to become conditional (you have to change first before I love you), in Marin, his love became more and more distant (love is not the point—just purify yourself to become a vehicle for impersonal love). Eventually the whole idea of love itself became an illusion (personal love is just two egos worshiping each other), and an ideology of impersonal enlightenment kicked in. But was there ever any real love at all?

Yet, from another perspective you could say that I was out for enlightenment, and Andrew's experiment of enlightened living seemed the best on the block at the time. I felt he was more exciting, more penetrating, than the other teachers that I had met. Andrew gave me very real and convincing spiritual experiences and his community was made up of people who were hell-bent for enlightenment just like me. As psychologist Len Oakes writes about the students of charismatic spiritual teachers, they are not washed out losers, gullible emotional weaklings, but sensitive and ambitious people who have some 'life work' in mind. They intuitively feel that the teacher can help them because he shares their values. As soon as they've completed their work, or feel they've received all they could get from the teacher, they leave.

In my case, I left when I felt I'd had enough. But at what point do you decide you've had enough? If you start to suspect the teacher's not good for you, what to do? How far do you go in battling Doubt, suspending judgment? At what point do you decide that the teacher is not worthy of your trust? The spiritual path is full of obstacles and challenges, your ego can be expected to come up with all kinds of doubts and malicious suspicions about the teacher. There is no proof that the teacher can give you the radical transformation that he promises. But you have to give it a fair chance. If you bail out prematurely you might miss out on the prize. Better be real sure before you bail out. Surely that's part of what kept me going for eleven years.

When people ask me whether I feel I've wasted eleven years of my life with Andrew, I tell them I wouldn't want to have missed them. I went for the greatest adventure I can imagine, the journey towards love and truth, and I sacrificed everything for it. It took me a long time to learn my lessons, but I'm sure that nothing was wasted.

* * *

The writing of this book has been a sobering process of soul-searching, of delving into some moments which were extremely painful, of redefining and understanding not only these eleven long years, but also my basic philosophy of life, my ideals. I don't feel personally angry anymore with Andrew or his community. Although I see Andrew's shortcomings more clearly and soberly, his adolescent all-or nothing mentality, his need for affirmation and power, I feel no need to go on a crusade against him.

But I feel saddened and concerned, and yes, sometimes angry when I hear continuing stories of abuse, and stories of how hard it is psychologically and emotionally for people to leave. When students do leave, they often find it difficult to speak of their experiences. Ex-students requested that I not mention their personal stories of abuse since they still find them too painful. As understandable as this is, it hurts when a spiritual community supposedly dedicated to the pursuit of truth has this kind of effect upon its members, even after they've left. It reminds me of the "conspiracy of silence" that is sometimes found among incest victims.

I've made this book as accurate and complete as possible, in the hope that it will contribute to opening up a dialogue, that it will encourage others to come forward with their stories, and that it will be of value to people who are looking for spiritual guidance. I feel it is a much-needed look behind the scenes that can serve as a sobering counterweight to many inspiring but abstract notions of what spirituality is and what it should look like. My story shows what it actually was and what it looked like.

9.2. Last Thoughts on Enlightenment

The notion of enlightenment remains a hard nut to crack. I no longer think enlightenment is a state of consciousness to be attained. Nor do I think it refers to a mystical union with some kind of transcendent Reality out there, the vessel of which we can become by purifying ourselves. To me it only makes sense to speak of a mystery that is not different from our self, the stuff we're made of. We can only realize this mystery by truly becoming who we already are and always have been, and this means embracing our individuality, not sacrificing it. If there is such a thing as enlightenment, I see it as an openness to all that exists, a willingness to let ourselves stand naked before life, allowing ourselves to be affected and overwhelmed. At the same time this openness to life must include our individuality, without needing to kill or suppress any part of it. The inherent paradox of striving for surrender, as well as the embodiment of self, means that we have to stretch in two opposite directions. Perhaps out of such a tension a beautiful human being can arise.

I joined Andrew's community out of a strong spiritual longing, a yearning for love and truth. I still pay tribute to this longing, it is part of who I am, who we all are. It is this longing for transcendence, for freedom, for overcoming our petty little selves, that Plato called Eros, Love. It might be temporarily satisfied by material possessions, by beautiful objects, or people that we love. Yet at heart this longing knows no boundaries and is never satisfied by any object. It is a longing for enlightenment.

How to give form to such a longing today? Is there any room for a postreligious spirituality? A postspiritual way of being? I feel that what I have learned is that our spiritual longing needs to be balanced by a healthy discrimination, a critical mind set, the courage to doubt. Eros needs to be balanced by healthy skepticism. Perhaps while wooing the eastern Goddess of Enlightenment we shouldn't forget the roots of our own western enlightenment:

"Enlightenment is man's emergence from his self-incurred immaturity. Immaturity is the inability to use one's own understanding without the guidance of another. This immaturity is self-incurred if its cause is not lack of understanding, but lack of resolution and courage to use it without the guidance of another. The motto of enlightenment is therefore: *Sapere aude!* Have courage to use your own understanding! "(Immanuel Kant, An Answer to the Question: "What is Enlightenment?" Königsberg in Prussia, 30th September, 1784).

And from another perspective you could say, maybe there's no need to search for enlightenment, maybe enlightenment is where you are. These days, I often feel, whether I'm sitting cross-legged on a meditation cushion, or jogging along the Amstel river near my house, a peace and contentment that is never far away, like a stream of running water just beneath the earth's surface. I feel more at home with myself than ever.